15 days
of prayer with
SAINT CLARE OF ASSISI

GW00750230

15 days
of prayer series

On a journey, it's good to have a guide. Even great saints took spiritual directors or confessors with them on their itineraries toward sanctity. Now you can be guided by the most influential spiritual figures of all time. The 15 Days of Prayer series introduces their deepest and most personal thoughts.

This popular series is perfect if you are looking for a gift, or if you want to be introduced to a particular guide and his or her spirituality. Each volume contains:

- ✄ A brief biography of the saint or spiritual leader
- ✄ A guide to creating a format for prayer or retreat
- ✄ Fifteen meditation sessions with focus points and reflection guides

15 days
of prayer with
SAINT CLARE OF ASSISI

Marie-France Becker

TRANSLATED BY
SR. PACELLI MILLANE

NEW CITY PRESS
Hyde Park, NY

A special word of thanks to
Jean-François Godet-Calogeras
for his kindness in reviewing the text
and for his helpful suggestions.
Also, my gratitude to
Gary Brandl and New City Press
for their promotion of
Franciscan texts and studies.

Published in the United States by New City Press
202 Comforter Blvd., Hyde Park, NY 12538
www.newcitypress.com
©2011 New City Press (English translation)

This book is a translation of *Prier 15 Jours avec Claire d'Assise*,
published by Nouvelle Cité, Montrouge, France.

Cover design by Durva Correia

Library of Congress Cataloging-in-Publication Data:

Becker, Marie-France.
  [Prier 15 jours avec Claire d'Assise. English]
  15 days of prayer with Saint Clare of Assisi / Marie-France Becker ;
translated by Pacelli Millane.
     p. cm.
  Includes bibliographical references (p.   ).
  ISBN 978-1-56548-371-2 (pbk. : alk. paper) 1. Clare, of Assisi, Saint,
1194-1253—Meditations. 2. Spiritual life—Catholic Church. I. Title.
II. Title: Fifteen days of prayer with Saint Clare of Assisi.
  BX4700.C6B4313 2011
  271'.97302—dc22
  [B]   2010050661

Printed in the United States of America

Contents

How to Use
This Book

An old Chinese proverb, or at least what I am able to recall of what is supposed to be an old Chinese proverb, goes something like this: "Even a journey of a thousand miles begins with a single step." When you think about it, the truth of the proverb is obvious. It is impossible to begin any project, let alone a journey, without taking the first step. I think it might also be true, although I cannot recall if another Chinese proverb says it, "that the first step is often the hardest." Or, as someone else once observed, "the distance between a thought and the corresponding action needed to implement the idea takes the most energy." I don't know who shared that perception with me but I am certain it was not an old Chinese master!

With this ancient proverbial wisdom, and the not-so-ancient wisdom of an unknown contemporary sage still fresh, we move from proverbs to presumptions. How do these relate to the task before us?

I am presuming that if you are reading this introduction it is because you are contemplating a journey. My presumption is that you are preparing for a spiritual journey and that you have taken at least some of the first steps necessary to prepare for this journey. I also presume, and please excuse me if I am making too many presumptions, that in your preparation for the spiritual journey you have determined that you need a guide. From deep within the recesses of your deepest self, there was something that called you to consider Saint Clare of Assisi as a potential companion. If my presumptions are correct, may I congratulate you on this decision? I think you have made a wise choice, a choice that can be confirmed by yet another source of wisdom, the wisdom that comes from practical experience.

Even an informal poll of experienced travelers will reveal a common opinion: it is very difficult to travel alone. Some might observe that it is even foolish. Still others may be even stronger in their opinion and go so far as to insist that it is necessary to have a guide, especially when you are traveling into uncharted waters and into territory that you have not yet experienced. I am of the personal opinion that a traveling companion is welcome under all circumstances. The thought of traveling alone, to some exciting destination without someone to share the journey with does not capture my imagination or channel my enthusiasm. However, with that being noted, what is simply a matter of preference on the normal journey becomes a matter of necessity when a person embarks on a spiritual journey.

The spiritual journey, which can be the most challenging of all journeys, is experienced best with a guide, a companion, or at the very least, a friend in whom you have placed your trust. This observation is not a preference or an opinion but rather an established spiritual necessity. All of the great saints with whom I am familiar had a spiritual director or a confessor who journeyed with them. Admittedly, at times the saints might well have traveled far beyond the experience of their guide and companion but more often than not they would return to their director and reflect on their experience. Understood in this sense, the director and companion provided a valuable contribution and necessary resource. When I was learning how to pray (a necessity for anyone who desires to be a full-time and public "religious person"), the community of men that I belong to gave me a great gift. Between my second and third year in college, I was given a one-year sabbatical, with all expenses paid and all of my personal needs met. This period of time was called novitiate. I was officially designated as a novice, a beginner in the spiritual journey, and I was assigned a "master," a person who was willing to lead me. In addition to the master, I was provided with every imaginable book and any other resource that I could possibly need. Even with all that I was provided, I did not learn how to pray because of the books and the unlimited resources, rather it was the master, the companion who was the key to the experience.

One day, after about three months of reading, of quiet and solitude, and of practicing all of the methods and descriptions of prayer that were available to me, the master called. "Put away the books, forget the method, and just listen." We went into a room, became quiet, and tried to recall the presence of God, and then, the master simply prayed out loud and permitted me to listen to his prayer. As he prayed, he revealed his hopes, his dreams, his struggles, his successes, and most of all, his relationship with God. I discovered as I listened that his prayer was deeply intimate but most of all it was self-revealing. As I learned about him, I was led through his life experience to the place where God dwells. At that moment I was able to understand a little bit about what I was supposed to do if I really wanted to pray.

The dynamic of what happened when the master called, invited me to listen, and then revealed his innermost self to me as he communicated with God in prayer, was important.

It wasn't so much that the master was trying to reveal to me what needed to be said; he was not inviting me to pray with the same words that he used, but rather that he was trying to bring me to that place within myself where prayer becomes possible. That place, a place of intimacy and of self-awareness, was a necessary stop on the journey and it was a place that I needed to be led to. I could not have easily discovered it on my own.

The purpose of the volume that you hold in your hand is to lead you, over a period of fifteen days or, maybe more realistically, fifteen prayer periods, to a place where prayer is possible. If you already have a regular experience and practice of prayer, perhaps this volume can help lead you to a deeper place, a more intimate relationship with the Lord.

It is important to note that the purpose of this book is not to lead you to a better relationship with Saint Clare of Assisi, your spiritual companion. Although your companion will invite you to share some of her deepest and most intimate thoughts, your companion is doing so only to bring you to that place where God dwells. After all, the true measurement of all companions for the journey is that they bring you to the place where you need to be, and then they step back, out of the picture. A guide who brings you to the desired destination and then sticks around is a very unwelcome guest!

Many times I have found myself attracted to a particular idea or method for accomplishing a task, only to discover that what seemed to be inviting and helpful possessed too many details. All of my energy went to the mastery of the details and I soon lost my enthusiasm. In each instance, the book that seemed so promising ended up on my bookshelf, gathering dust. I can assure you, it is not our intention that this book end up in your bookcase, filled with promise, but unable to deliver.

There are three simple rules that need to be followed in order to use this book with a measure of satisfaction.

Place: It is important that you choose a place for reading that provides the necessary atmosphere for reflection and that does not allow for too many distractions. Whatever place you choose needs to be comfortable, have the necessary lighting, and, finally, have a sense of "welcoming" about it. You need to be able to look forward to the experience of the journey. Don't travel steerage if you know you will be more comfortable in first class and if the choice is realistic for you. On the other hand, if first class is a distraction and you feel more comfortable and more yourself in steerage, then it is in steerage that you belong.

My favorite place is an overstuffed and comfortable chair in my bedroom. There is a light over my shoulder, and the chair reclines if I feel a need to recline. Once in a while, I get lucky and the sun comes through my window and bathes the entire room in light. I have other options and other places that are available to me but this is the place that I prefer.

Time: Choose a time during the day when you are most alert and when you are most receptive to reflection, meditation, and prayer. The time that you choose is an essential component. If you are a morning person, for example, you should choose a time that is in the morning. If you are more alert in the afternoon, choose an afternoon time slot; and if evening is your preference, then by all means choose the evening. Try to avoid "peak" periods in your daily routine when you know that you might be disturbed. The time that you choose needs to be your time and needs to work for you.

It is also important that you choose how much time you will spend with your companion each day. For some it will be possible to set aside enough time in order to read and reflect on all the material that is offered for a given day. For others, it might not be possible to devote one time to the suggested material for the day, so the prayer period may need to be extended for two, three, or even more sessions. It is not important how long it takes you; it is only important that

it works for you and that you remain committed
to that which is possible.

Freedom: It may seem strange to suggest that
freedom is the third necessary ingredient, but
I have discovered that it is most important. By
freedom I understand a certain "stance toward
life," a "permission to be myself and to be
gentle and understanding of who I am." I am
constantly amazed at how the human person so
easily sets himself or herself up for disappoint-
ment and perceived failure. We so easily make
judgments about ourselves and our actions and
our choices, and very often those judgments are
negative, and not at all helpful.

For instance, what does it really matter if
I have chosen a place and a time, and I have
missed both the place and the time for three
days in a row? What does it matter if I have chosen, in that twilight time before I am completely
awake and still a little sleepy, to roll over and
to sleep for fifteen minutes more? Does it mean
that I am not serious about the journey, that I
really don't want to pray, that I am just fooling
myself when I say that my prayer time is important to me? Perhaps, but I prefer to believe that it
simply means that I am tired and I just wanted a
little more sleep. It doesn't mean anything more
than that. However, if I make it mean more than
that, then I can become discouraged, frustrated,
and put myself into a state where I might more

easily give up. "What's the use? I might as well forget all about it."

The same sense of freedom applies to the reading and the praying of this text. If I do not find the introduction to each day helpful, I don't need to read it. If I find the questions for reflection at the end of the appointed day repetitive, then I should choose to close the book and go my own way. Even if I discover that the reflection offered for the day is not the one that I prefer and that the one for the next day seems more inviting, then by all means, go on to the one for the next day.

That's it! If you apply these simple rules to your journey you should receive the maximum benefit and you will soon find yourself at your destination. But be prepared to be surprised. If you have never been on a spiritual journey you should know that the "travel brochures" and the other descriptions that you might have heard are nothing compared to the real thing. There is so much more than you can imagine.

A final prayer of blessing suggests itself:

> Lord, catch me off guard today.
> Surprise me with some moment of
>   beauty or pain
> So that at least for the moment
> I may be startled into seeing that you
>   are here in all your splendor,
> Always and everywhere,

Barely hidden,
Beneath,
Beyond,
Within this life I breathe.

Frederick Buechner

Rev. Thomas M. Santa, CSsR
Liguori, Missouri

Presentation of Sources

Letters to Agnes

A gnes of Prague, daughter of the King of Bohemia, founded a monastery of Poor Sisters where she will enter. From Agnes's correspondence with Clare of Assisi, we have four of Clare's letters within which she, while encouraging Agnes on her path of the spiritual life, shares her own experience with us. A strong friendship, sealed in the poor and crucified Christ, unites these two women who never met.

Testament and Blessing

In her *Testament* written near the end of her life, Clare expresses a double fidelity: fidelity to Francis and to Lady Poverty. In this text she recounts the marvels which God accomplished in her life, then she offers a word of blessing to her sisters.

Form of Life of Clare

Clare struggles all her life to obtain a *Form of Life* conformed to her proposal. Two days before her death, she receives its approbation from the

Pope. The first Rule written by a woman for
women, this text is striking by its realism, its dem-
ocratic sense and its liberty regarding its sources.

Letter to Ermentrude

We know that Clare wrote two letters to a
certain Ermentrude of Bruges who founded
many monasteries in Flanders and who wanted
to live in the manner of the Poor Sisters of
Saint Damian. The text, which we have, could
be a compilation of these two messages.

Process of Canonization

This text, an account of the inquiry on the
life of Clare, reveals how she translated the
Gospel in a very concrete manner throughout
her existence. The Sisters who have lived with
Clare, four other persons who have known her
and her family, all testify under oath and, thus,
witness to the holiness of her life.

Life of Clare by Thomas of Celano

At the request of the Pope, Brother Thomas
of Celano writes Clare's life. To do this he uses
the *Process of Canonization* and questions some
brothers and sisters who have known Clare.

Abbreviations

1LAg	First Letter to Blessed Agnes of Prague (1234)
2LAg	Second Letter to Blessed Agnes of Prague (1235)
3LAg	Third Letter to Blessed Agnes of Prague (1238)
4LAg	Fourth Letter to Blessed Agnes of Prague (1253)
TestCl	Testament of Clare of Assisi
FlCl	Form of Life of Clare of Assisi
BlCl	Blessing of Clare of Assisi
LEr	Letter to Ermentrude of Bruges
PC	Acts of the Process of Canonization (1253)
BC	Bull of Canonization, Alexander IV (1255)
LegCl	Legend of Saint Clare (1254–1255)
1Cel	Life of Blessed Francis by Thomas of Celano (1228)
2Cel	Remembrance of the Desire of a Soul by Thomas of Celano (1245–1247)

The texts are generally taken from *The Lady: Clare of Assisi* for the writings of Clare and of Francis. However, to facilitate a prayerful reading, the translation is adapted by the translator. The Scripture texts are taken from the Jerusalem Bible.

Chronology

1193–94   After having received in prayer, an assurance of her safe delivery, Ortulana gives birth to a daughter, Clare, whose father's name is Favorone di Offreduccio. In Assisi, Italy, two other daughters, Catherine and Beatrice, will be born later.

1199   The Offreduccio women and children are obliged to live in exile in Perugia for several years during the political struggle within Assisi, that is, until after the battle of Collestrada in 1202.

1206   Francis' conversion; his prayer before the crucifix of San Damiano; he repairs three Churches including that of San Damiano.

1209   Pope Innocent III orally approves the new project presented to him by Francis of Assisi and the early Brothers, that is, to live the Gospel life of poverty and to *not extinguish the Spirit of holy prayer and devotion.*

1210   Clare hears Brother Francis of Assisi
        preach. She goes with a companion,
        Bona, to encounter him and he teaches
        her the way of Gospel poverty.

1212   On Palm Sunday, Clare makes her flight
        to the Portiuncula to be received by
        Francis and the Brothers before going to
        the Benedictine Monastery, San Paolo
        in Bastia. A few days later her family
        strongly contests her departure.

1212   Thus, Francis and some Brothers
        accompany Clare from San Paolo to
        Sant' Angelo of Panzo where her sis-
        ter Catherine (later Francis changes
        her name to Agnes) will join her.

1212   Clare and her sister Agnes move defini-
        tively to San Damiano, where they are
        rapidly joined by other women. Later,
        these women will be called the *Order of
        Saint Damian* (the Damianites).

1214   Sister Balvina, one of Clare's com-
        panion creates a new community in
        Spello.

1215   Francis gives a *Form of Life* to the
        Poor Ladies of San Damiano.
        *Because by divine inspiration you have
        made yourselves daughters and hand-
        maids of the most High, most Exalted*

King, the heavenly Father, and have taken the Holy Spirit as your spouse, choosing to live according to the perfection of the holy Gospel, I resolve and promise for myself and for my brothers always to have the same loving care and special solicitude for you as for them.

At the request of Francis and of the Bishop, Clare accepts the role of Abbess of San Damiano.

1217   Cardinal Hugolino arrives in Tuscany as Papal legate for the religious women and in 1219, he issues *Constitutions* based on the *Rule of Saint Benedict*, omitting poverty and a relationship with the Friars Minor.

1219   Sister Agnes is sent as Abbess to Monticello near Florence. Tradition states the first foundation in France is at Reims in 1220.

1224   The beginning of Clare's long illness. Francis receives the stigmata at LaVerna.

1225   Text given to the Poor Ladies by Francis of Assisi before his death.

Listen, little poor ones called by the Lord, who have come together from many parts and provinces. Live always

*in truth, that you may die in obedience.
Do not look at the life outside, for that
of the Spirit is better.*

1226   On October 4th, the death of Francis.
His body is brought to San Damiano
for viewing by Clare and the Sisters.

1227   Pope Gregory IX (Hugolino) wants
to dispense Clare from her ideals
of poverty and removes the Friars
Minor as chaplains.

1228   Gregory IX grants the *Privilege of
Poverty* to the Sisters at San Damiano.
An acclamation of the project of
Clare in the official *Legend* of Thomas
of Celano on the *Life of Saint Francis*:
*A noble structure of precious pearls arose
above this woman, whose praise comes not
from mortals but from God. Forty or fifty
of them can dwell together in one place,
forming one spirit in them out of many.*

1230   Agnes, the daughter of the King of
Bohemia, begins a monastery in
Prague.

1234   Clare of Assisi's first letter of correspondence with Agnes of Prague.
*What a great and praiseworthy exchange:
to receive the hundred-fold in place of one,
and to possess eternal life.*

1234   Fifty Poor Ladies of San Damiano
            sign a civil document establishing a
            procurator to sell some land given to
            the Sisters. Thus, we know the names
            of fifty Sisters who lived in the primi-
            tive community at San Damiano.

1235   Second Letter of Clare of Assisi to
            Agnes of Prague.
                *May you go forward securely, joyfully,
            and swiftly, on the path of prudent hap-
            piness, believing nothing, agreeing with
            nothing that would dissuade you from
            this commitment.*

1238   Third Letter of Clare of Assisi to
            Agnes of Prague.
                *Through contemplation, transform your
            entire being into the image of the Godhead
            Itself, so that you too may feel what friends
            feel in tasting the hidden sweetness that,
            from the beginning, God Himself has
            reserved for His lovers.*

1240   Saracens invade the Monastery of
            San Damiano. Miraculous protec-
            tion of the community. A year later,
            another miracle of the liberation of
            the city of Assisi from Vitale d'Aversa
            on June 22 by the intercessory prayers
            of the Sisters of San Damiano.

1247   Change of affiliation of Rules issued by Innocent IV. The Constitutions of Innocent IV affiliates the Damianites with the *Rule of Francis of Assisi*. Mention of the *Rule of Saint Benedict* is deleted.

1250   Pope Innocent IV declares that Poor Ladies are not bound to his *Constitutions* and leaves them free to chose among the various texts. Clare and the Sisters of San Damiano begin to formulate a new *Form of Life*. Cardinal Raynaldus approves this *Form of Life* on September 16, 1252.

1253   Fourth and last known letter to Agnes of Prague.

     Gaze upon that mirror each day, O Queen and Spouse of Jesus Christ, and continually study your face in it.

1253   Pope Innocent IV visits Clare in Assisi before her death. Clare's *Form of Life* is approved by a Papal Bull "*Solet annure*" on August 9th. *The Form of Life of the Order of the Poor Sisters that Blessed Francis established is this: to observe the Holy Gospel of our Lord Jesus Christ.*

1253   *"Go calmly in peace, because you will
            have a good escort. The One Who cre-
            ated you has sent you the Holy Spirit."*
            Clare dies at San Damiano on
            August 11th. Pope Innocent IV pre-
            sides at her funeral.

1253   Clare is buried in Church of San
            Giorgo in Assisi. On October 18th,
            Innocent IV orders an inquiry into
            the virtues and miracles of Clare's
            life. In November, Clare's sister,
            Agnes of Assisi, dies.

1253   November 24th – 29th. Testimonies
            are given on the holiness of Clare
            of Assisi by fifteen Sisters of San
            Damiano. There is a unanimous
            accord of her holiness by the Abbess
            and assembled Sisters as well as by
            five other lay witnesses. These tes-
            timonies will become the *Acts of the
            Process of Canonization.*

1254–55   Writing of the *Versified Legend of the
            Virgin Clare.*

1255   August 15th. Clare is canonized by
            Pope Alexander IV (Raynaldus) and
            he orders the composition of the
            official *biography, Legend of St. Clare.*

Clare brilliant by her merits, by the brightness of her sublime miracles on earth, shines brilliantly. Clare was silent, yet her fame was proclaimed.

1260   Clare's body is transferred from San Giorgo to the Basilica of Saint Clare.

1263   The name of the *Order of Saint Damian* is changed to the *Order of Saint Clare*.

A Fountain of Light

*T*he streets of Assisi still buzz with rumors of the final fantasies of Francis, the son of Peter Bernardone: that is, how he put himself at the service of the lepers, lavishing care on them and begging their food. Clare of Offreduccio, who is sixteen or seventeen years old, listens with interest to the stories of her cousin, Rufino: Called by the words of the Gospel which invite to follow the footprints of Jesus, to sell everything for the poor and to announce peace, Francis, himself, cried out: *This is what I seek, this is what I desire with all my heart. He did not delay before he devoutly began to put into effect what he heard (1Cel 22).*

Both social rank and culture separate Clare from this merchant's son. She is a "lady," daughter of the Knight Offreduccio of Favarone, noble of the city, and of Lady Ortulana.

Born in 1193, she has received the name, new to this era, of Clare. For her mother, pregnant and near the time of delivery, was praying one day in a Church before the Crucifix and was asking the grace of a blessed deliverance, when she heard a voice say to her: *Do not be afraid, woman, for you will give birth in safety to a light which will give light more clearly than light itself* (*LegCl* 2).

Clare *learns to know God from her mother. She freely stretched out her hands to the poor and satisfied the needs of many out of the abundance of her house* (*LegCl* 3). In the paternal home, the education conforms to her rank, develops her natural qualities of refinement, of goodness and of strength. But she has equally grown-up in a violent and heavy atmosphere of a city under the stress of war and all sorts of rivalry. The Commune of Assisi searched to free itself from the feudal Lords; and Clare must flee to Perugia for some years.

She returns to her city. She can only try to separate herself from the feudal society. Only one name dwells in her heart, that of the Lord Jesus. A single desire burns her: to live the Gospel after the example of Francis. In listening to his preaching in the Cathedral of Saint Rufino, she feels a profound complicity awaken between her and this new fool of God. His words have touched her heart and she ardently wished to encounter him. As Francis, she desires to give her life totally to the Lord Jesus, to vow to Him her body and her heart. If her parents dream of a good marriage for her, she remains unshakable in her decision. In the course of her encounters with Francis, she is more and more encouraged in her choice. At the heart of this friendship, which progressively binds them, they share the fire which lives in them: the love of this poor God who came hidden in the history of humanity.

Palm Sunday evening, 1212, robed in her most beautiful clothes, her biographer tells us that she fled by the death door of her home, signifying how much she wants to follow Jesus in His route of the Passion and *return love for love*, the One who has loved her so much (cf. *LegCl* 30–32). By this audacious liberty does she not make proof of it by leaving her paternal home in the countryside of Assisi to find Francis and his brothers, whose strange manner of living is widely talked about in the city! Nothing can weaken the determination and the courage with which she comes to conquer all the oppositions. Her womanly heart has no other desire than to conquer *through love for this God placed poor in the crib, lived poor in the world and remained naked on the cross* (*TestCl* 45). All her life, her tenacity finds support in fidelity to this profound call: *As a poor virgin, embrace the poor Christ* (*2LAg* 18).

Francis consecrates her to the Lord by clothing her in the habit of poverty and in cutting her hair. During fifteen days, she stays with the Benedictines of Saint Paul at Bastia. But their form of life, despite their cordial welcome, leaves her unsatisfied. She has nostalgia for the poor life that Jesus led and of which Francis and his brothers show her the example. She leaves the Benedictines to join the women living in community, in penance and prayer at Saint Angelo di Panzo on the slopes of Subasio.

Even there, Clare feels the pressing invitation to live differently and does not find peace of soul. Following the counsel of Francis, she leaves for Saint Damian, a small chapel belonging to the Bishop of Assisi and which Francis rebuilt with his hands. It is there that she definitively settles and gives birth to the Order of the Poor Sisters, better known as the Poor Clares. *The Lord gives her some sisters so that together they are faithful to love and adore Him* (*BC* 6). Francis writes them a short *Form of Life* which puts the accent on poverty according to the Gospel and the sisters belong to the Order of brothers.

In the great happiness of possessing nothing, Clare and her sisters lead a marvelous and laborious existence. Before Christ crucified, who spoke to Francis inviting him to repair the Church, they elevate the praise of their hearts toward God and prostrating, adore Him. They give themselves to modest works, which is the lot of the little ones, and through these, they commune with the humility of God of Whom they want to follow the traces of poverty, simplicity and love.

To glorify the Father in His holy Church, Clare encounters many obstacles. In 1215, the Lateran Council forbids all new Rules of religious life. Clare must, thereafter, adopt that of Benedict,

and Francis uses all of his authority so that
she accepts the title of Abbess. Thus begins for
Clare a long struggle to obtain from the Church,
the right to live poor and without revenue. It
was, in effect, foolhardy in the changing feudal
society to lead a religious life in abandoning
oneself with confidence to the *Father of Mercies*.
A minimum of security was required for a
group of pious women to live decently and the
monasteries benefited from titles and privileges
to subsist. The originality of Clare has been to
maintain her religious family on the "nothing-
ness of poverty." For that, she ardently refuses
all privilege, if this is not the one that with an
audacious perseverance, she solicits from the
Pope himself, the *Privilege of Poverty*, and the
privilege to possess nothing. This weighty, and
completely original, demand surprises Innocent
III and history tells us that he was amused by it.
*The Pope himself with great joy wrote with his own
hand the first draft of the privilege (LegCl 14).*

Shortly, other monasteries adopted the
current mode of life at Saint Damian and the
Pope names Cardinal Hugolino, protector of
these new communities. He imposed on the
sisters a *Rule of Life*: of new observances, very
strict in the domain of the cloister, of silence, of
fasting and some mortification. But neither Clare
nor Francis have taken part in the elaboration of
this text which remains totally silent on poverty
and belonging to the family of the Friars Minors.

In his solicitude toward Clare and her sisters, Cardinal Hugolino, who will become Pope Gregory IX, tried to make Clare go back on her will to live poverty. But in her restlessness before the precariousness of their means of subsistence, Clare never ceases to oppose his will so as to follow Christ.

August 6, 1247, Pope Innocent IV, gives a new Rule to the Poor Sisters. *The Rule of Francis* is the juridical base for it, but it does not make any mention of the *Privilege of Poverty.* Clare remains unsatisfied and determines to write her own Rule. After an experience of more than forty years of life at Saint Damian, she composes it, inspired by the structure and contents of the *Rule of Francis*, and integrating with wisdom some elements of the *Rules of Benedict, Hugolino* and *Innocent.* Near to her death, August 9, 1253, Clare received the *Bull* of approbation of this *Rule.*

It is a cry of gratitude to the One *who has guided her and made her holy*, that on August 11, 1253, she enters into the land of the living after having lived as "pilgrim and stranger" in this world, leading until the end, with an audacious tenacity and a joyous confidence, the combat of poverty. August 15, 1255, Pope Alexander IV canonized her, celebrating her as *a pure source and a new fountain of living water, for the refreshment and comfort of souls* (*BC* 11).

Become What You Contemplate

*T*his book would like to trace or at least outline a path of prayer. Such a path can be imagined in different ways. One could strive to mark out a journey toward God. It could be a question of determining the stages of a voyage, of a one-way trip between a well-known point of departure and a planned objective. This is an invitation to leave the place where you are and try to arrive somewhere else in fifteen days.

But we would like to pass these fifteen days with Clare of Assisi. She leads us, it is true, in a quest of God. To walk beside her, is to begin. And more than a walk! The search for God often takes the pace of a light walk. At the same time, however, our companion on the road is a sedentary. During more than forty years, she lived in the same Monastery of Saint Damian, giving herself to very ordinary tasks without display. Also, with such a woman, this way of prayer resembles, rather, a promenade in the field, which escorts someone to the point of

departure, but brings them back different and
enriched. It is not a question to leave the everyday to go to God, but that the everyday is carried into the prayer by accepting that God sends
us there and to work as he wishes.

Such a promenade, to be fruitful, supposes
a curiosity. Some days before her death, Clare
invites some brothers to her bedside to read
to her some passages of Holy Scripture. *When
Brother Juniper appeared among them, that excel-
lent jester of the Lord who uttered the Lord's words
which were often warming, Clare was filled with a
new joy and asked him if he had had anything new
from the Lord* (*LegCl* 45). Fifteen days of prayer
with Clare, is it not, day after day to make the
same untiring request: "Today, what can you
teach me about God?" Or if you prefer: What
is it that I pray today? The title of each of the
fifteen chapters of this book presents an element
of response to this question.

There it is, painted with broad strokes, the
journey of our walk with Clare. But let's allow
this outing the right to reserve some surprises. It
is part of the most simple realities of our life that
we set out on the route. Life is too abundant to
force oneself to make clear classifications. Clare
has not written a treatise on prayer which would
be sufficient for us to read and to comment. In
the varied collection of her writings (*Letters,
Testament, Rule, Benediction*) we will glean from
some revealing texts that which captivated her

and that she selected each day as the unique
Good News capable of allowing her to chant
her existence: the mystery of the poor Christ.
We will risk betraying their author by imposing
on them a plan too rigid. That we will allow
ourselves from time to time to be distracted,
every now and then, by an unforeseen passage,
by crooked paths, by some near blossoms which
invite us to stop.... Nothing of that will seri-
ously detour from our project: to contemplate
the God of Clare and, in this contemplation,
allow Him to transform our gaze on Him, on
us, on our surroundings and our daily savor.

1
Receive from God and Trust in Him

Focus Point

////////////////

Clare, this woman who accompanies us in our search for God, goes forth in life even to the threshold of death with a heart full of gratitude to the One who created her, makes her holy and guides her with assurance. All of her existence unfolds in the good will of the Creator and the reception of this blessing is momentum on the road.

////////////////

The most holy virgin, Clare, speaks within herself and silently addresses her soul. "Go without anxiety," she said, "for you have a good escort for your journey. Go," she says, "for He who created you has made you holy. And, always protecting you as a mother does her child; He has loved you with a tender

love. May you be blessed, O Lord," she says,
"you who have created my soul!"

When one of the Sisters asks her to whom
she is speaking, she replied: "I am speaking
to my blessed soul." That glorious escort was
not standing afar off. So turning to another
daughter she says: "Do you see, O child, the
King of glory whom I see?"

(LegCl 46)

///////////////

Blessed Are You, Who Have Created Me

*T*o approach our way of prayer we begin, in some ways, with the conclusion. Here the biography of Clare evokes her last moments and her last words. Often the last words of a person bind together the essential realities which underlie her existence. Thus, it's Clare's whole life that we embrace in a single gaze while praying today the words of her last breath. And these are words of blessing and marvelous praise of God the Creator. From Him, Clare has received each moment of her life. From Him, she receives everything.

In her *Testament,* this grateful welcome of the Creator blossoms under the form of another blessing, destined for all her Sisters. The love which gives Clare existence and of which she knows herself as a debtor, becomes a fountain in her own heart. She can not welcome and bless Life without letting it stream forth, through her, with the same superabundance to each of her sisters.

To pray with Clare, therefore, is to discover oneself enveloped by the liberating song of two blessings. They are like an echo throughout her whole life.

That which we pray on this first day is the indelible trace of a profound attitude of poverty and of dispossession facing the creating goodness. It is the astonishment before a Presence who calls us into existence and before a Love who desires to create us by clothing us again with His beauty and benevolence.

Clare recognizes the Giver of all good, who gladdens her being with jubilation and enables her to go forth from herself, in order to live from Him and for Him. Likewise, her praise is her respiration. Her heart is free there; her gaze on others and on life is full of respect and optimism. In this last cry of gladness, she shares the fullness of her faith with us. Without complex, she recognizes herself adorned with the beauty of God and can exclaim with the psalmist: *I am wonderfully made, wonderful are your works* (*Ps* 138:14). Clare repeats God's admiration on the first morning of the world, when contemplating His creation; He saw that it was good.

I beg you in the Lord to praise the Lord by your very life, Clare writes to Agnes (*3LAg* 41). *We are greatly bound to bless and praise God* (*TestCl* 22); such is the fundamental attitude of all faith which trans-

forms life into a momentum of praise toward
the Source of all good. The blessing of Clare, on
the eve of her death, is the accomplished expression of the marvel of living of a woman dazzled
by love of which she is the object.

The One Who Created You
Has also Sanctified You

Clare knows the work of God. In her song
of gratitude, she does not deny any of her history and she does not want to put any moment
in parenthesis. However, the trials have not
been lacking, we have recalled them, but she
accepts who she is in the depths of herself. In
the same movement, she welcomes all of her
past and receives, in confidence, the future still
hidden in God.

To which harmony, to which faith, to which
interior poverty also, must she come to gather
again the totality of her existence in the hollow
of her hands and to return it to her Creator with
a chant of blessing on her lips! This consent, this
courageous and serene submission to the real,
becomes a source of peace and a path of communion with God.

Clare knows it: *the One, who has created her, has
made her holy*. Unceasingly, He has enveloped
her with His tender mercy. In this, she finds
her total assurance. The reconciliation with the
darkest part of our history, living of struggles,
of victories, of joys, of strong aversions and of

loves, become little by little the fertile ground where the word of blessing is born and in which we will abandon ourselves to the Father. Praise and thanksgiving place us in the truth of who, sometimes, we are: disfigured creatures, often wounded but loved, while receiving the grace of being and of rebirth each moment.

You Have a Good Guide for the Road

Clare's final prayer witnesses to the breath which has carried her: an uninterrupted wonder for the life received from her Creator and a total abandon to God who accompanies her during these days. Throughout our entire daily life something is revealed of the face of God, of His unheard of proximity and of His call. Within the agitated and sorrowful history of the world, in the quest of justice and peace and the thirst for happiness which torments us, we are continually invited to let God's strength be revealed. Clare names him, *Father of Mercies, giver of all gifts, past, present and to come (TestCl* 2). The tenderness of such a Father, can it be lacking in the one who placed her hand in his for the road? Clare abandons herself in security to the good guide whose presence remains faithful.

Clare does not dream of God. For her, the Creator has a face, that of Jesus, the *poor Crucified* (*1LAg* 13). To bless God is to give thanks for the gift of a good guide, the Son of God Himself,

Icon of the goodness of the Father. All of her life, she has desired to follow the poverty, humility and holy simplicity of the Lord Jesus. Coming to terms, she marvels at the happiness which has opened in her this presence of the poor God. This was a gracious gift, not owed, which dilates her heart to reveal the infinite dimension of the present given to her. From this experienced *guide*, she has received the tenacious assurance and the tranquil force which have permitted her, day after day, to live in the risk of the Gospel. Christ, her guide, *has loved her with a tender love as a mother loves her son. Can a woman forget her baby at the breast? Even if these were to forget, I shall not forget you* (*Is* 49:15). Jesus has held to His promise: *I will always protect you* (*LegCl* 22).

The heart, which receives from God, is in security. It no longer has other desires than to live in the confidence of the One who keeps it in existence with maternal tenderness. Then, why fear? How can we not marvel at the miracle of being in the land of the living?

The blessing is not a passive prayer. It's an invitation to take to the road: to consent to be loved *"free of charge,"* to receive from Another who desires us to be in covenant with Him, to be reconciled, to be confident with the burden of all reality and to walk joyfully in the presence of this divine guide, God, Father, Son and Spirit. "To bless and to trust" is the savory fruit of a poor heart: a heart passionately loving this God who is burning with love for His creature and a heart radically surrendered to the One who gives and is given without measure.

Reflection Questions

Are you aware of being a creature? How is this manifest in your life? Which feelings afflict you, face to face with your Creator? Is the prayer of praise and blessing familiar to you? Difficult? Why? How are you creative in your own life?

2
Receive God from Others

Focus Point

////////////

At the beginning of Clare's journey, Francis, a man passionate for the Gospel and a lover of the poor Jesus, knew Clare's secret desire and led her discretely in her own choices by some counsels. Together they gazed toward God, who came to inflame our humanity with love, and their friendship is the most precious place where folly stammers, even in the heart of God.

////////////

The Son of God has become for us the Way that our blessed father Francis, His true lover and imitator, has shown and taught us by word and example.

Therefore, beloved sisters, we must consider the immense gifts that God has bestowed on us, but among others, those that He has seen fit to work in us through His

44

beloved servant, our blessed father Francis,
not only after our conversion but also while
we were still in the unhappy vanity of the
world. In fact, almost immediately after his
conversion, when the holy man did not as yet
have brothers or companions, while building
the church of San Damiano, where he was
totally visited by divine consolation and
impelled to abandon the world, completely
through great joy and the enlightenment
of the Holy Spirit, the holy man made a
prophecy about us that the Lord later fulfilled.

Climbing the wall of that church, he
shouted in French to some poor people who
were standing nearby: Come and help me in
the work on the monastery of San Damiano,
because there will as yet be ladies here who
will glorify our heavenly Father throughout
His holy, universal Church by their celebrated
and holy manner of life.

(TestCl 5–14)

///////////

*C*lare rereads her existence in order to
glean the essential of what she wishes to
bequeath to her sisters, the treasure which can
neither be lost nor squandered. From this woman's heart, Francis's name arises, rich memories,
of starry hours, blessed and engraved, which
enlighten the long struggle undertaken to persevere in the way of the *highest poverty*. The pas-

sionate thrust of a double fidelity has cheerfully kept her course toward God: fidelity to Francis and fidelity to Lady Poverty. This gives birth to a happiness which finds expression in a profound gratitude toward the *Father of Mercies*.

Francis, Sacrament of God

God finds his joy in speaking to us in human tenderness. He chooses some persons and murmurs some names where he deposits his grace. In them, he hopes that we will interpret the signs of his unique love. For Clare, the grace of God is given to hear, to touch, to contemplate in this son of the merchant of Assisi who allowed himself to burn with the fire of the Gospel. In the poetry of the life of Francis, Clare discovers the poetry of her own existence. In her attachment to the little poor man, she binds herself to the poor Jesus who seduces her heart and in her love for the Son of God; she sings her love for Francis. Francis is a present, a gift of God and a grace among graces.

Francis, the Prophet

Such a friendship is an opening and a communion to the unique call of the Spirit. When Francis rebuilds the Church of Saint Damian, a luminous intuition of the Spirit leads him toward Clare and her sisters. Under this impulsion, the little poor man announces the birth of the Order of the Poor Sisters who will live the same charism as his. Clare gives form to this prophecy in becoming the first stone of a community who is in love with the *poor Crucified.* After having restored the little chapel, Francis offers to the Priest in charge, the necessary money to buy oil for the perpetual lamp. Thus, to which lamp of the sanctuary did he dream? Clare and her sisters are they not the lamp and the true oil who honor the image of the Crucified? By the fidelity of their presence at Saint Damian, they fulfill the desire of Francis.

Francis, the Guide

If the *Most High Heavenly Father, through his mercy and his grace*, enlightens the heart of Clare, Francis, *by word and example, shows the Way* (*TestCl* 5, 24). He is the voice that announces the Way. Clare discerns, without hesitation, the very concrete route that he borrows to reveal to her, her personal way: *God saw fit to speak these words about our vocation and election* (*TestCl* 16).

Like a lamp on her road, the words of Francis profoundly engraved in her memory enlighten her own development, nourish her desire and uphold her momentum. Her heart never remains deaf when he exhorts her throughout her life to give birth to her vocation, *the greatest of all graces* (*TestCl* 2–4).

The *good guide for the road,* to whom she abandons herself in confidence, takes the face of this new fool of God who shares with her the same passion for Jesus. From him, she receives God in whom she discovers the traits which touch her heart and put her on the way toward a life of a Poor Sister. The contagious strength of his examples, the persuasive quality of his voice, the loving ardor which places Francis in the following of the poor and humble Jesus, leads Clare in the footprints of the Most High Son of God. Francis shows her the way of true humanization as well as the plenitude toward which she tends and which Francis himself describes thus: *Because by divine inspiration you have made yourselves daughters and handmaids of the most Exalted King, the heavenly Father, and have taken the Holy Spirit as your spouse (RegCl 6:3).*

Francis, the Gardener

Francis pledges himself to take attentive care of Clare and of her sisters and to surround them with a special solicitude. He is given by the Lord to the Community of Saint Damian as *founder, planter, and helper in the service of Christ (TestCl 48).* Clare recognizes it with emotion: *Who while he was living was always solicitous in word and in deed to cherish and take care of us, his plant (TestCl 49).* He was *our pillar, [our] only consolation after God and [our] support (TestCl 38).*

Little plant of Francis, Clare lives from the same vigor and breathes the same breath of evangelical freshness. He remains for her, the gardener of her spiritual growth. As for Francis, he welcomes his sister as the well-matched aid that the Creator gave to Adam in the morning of Genesis. Clare remains for him the mirror of what he is called to live among his brothers on the paths of Umbria. With her companions she will keep watch until the end over the fire that the Spirit himself lit in the heart of the son of Peter Bernardone, flinging him on the roads of the world to weep for the Love who is not loved.

In the faith and love which inhabits them, Clare and Francis take refuge in each other. Running the same adventure, each one tastes the happiness to see the love of the Lord grow in the other. Together, penetrating into the mystery of the inexpressible love of Jesus crucified, they know an astonishing communion woven from gratitude of fervor, of admiration and of affection. Neither distance nor death is able to break it. In a love, free from every instinct of possession, they awaken, one for the other, this tranquil assurance and strong tenderness, footprints of the God of heaven in our human histories. At the heart of the unshakeable attachment of these two beings, the unlimited space designs a love without measure where each one receives God Himself from the other. Their communion opens them to the true liberty where the face of being loved is not a screen, but access to the infinite horizon of God. Each one became for the other, an icon of the Beloved, an icon of God, near and *Most High*, who finds his joy in the happiness of his children and of whom the grandeur is to hide Himself in the faces of others.

Reflection Questions

In the path of the believer, mediators are precious. Have you known men or women who opened new horizons for you in your spiritual life? Try to remember a decisive encounter at a given moment of your existence. For which reality of your life would you like the support and the prayer of others? What conditions are required for a friendship to be "spiritual"?

3
Cling to God

Focus Point

"Always remember your beginning," this will not allow us to waste our life in familiar routines. The footprints of yesterday allow us to pose those of today and tomorrow with confidence and courage to triumph over obstacles.

The attachment to Jesus is not burdensome slavery, but loving freedom. In it, life becomes a light race and in this bond of love, of which neither person nor anything can separate us, we advance serenely on the path of happiness.

For love of Him to Whom you have offered yourself as a holy and pleasing sacrifice, that you always be mindful of your commitment like another Rachel always seeing your beginning.

51

What you hold, may you hold,
What you do, may you do and not stop.
   But with swift pace, light step,
      unswerving feet,
      So that even your steps stir up no dust,
   May you go forward
      Securely, joyfully and swiftly,
      On the path of prudent happiness
                        (2LAg 10b–13)

Always Remember Your Beginning

Writing to her friend, Agnes, Clare urges her to remember her first call: it contains the light to illumine the road on which to travel and the breath to strengthen her momentum. To look again at her history rejoins the fundamental attitude of all prayer by which, peacefully, under the gaze of God, we gather a living spray of the founding events of our spiritual experience and the creative words of the Lord which orient our existence from the beginning.

The place of memory offers an invigorating pause where the powers of the heart give impetus to desire. Always *remember....* Clare does not invite us to a nostalgic withdrawal into the past of our initial encounter with the Lord. It is a question of drawing forth a new momentum in our journey toward him. The beginning is before us and creates a call.

Always remembering the marvels of God in our lives is the best manner of placing ourselves in the presence of his love offered today because it is given forever. It is him who calls us to live in covenant and it is, also, him who gives *a good beginning, may give the increase and may also give final perseverance* (*TestCl* 78).

Remember in the days of obscurity, so as to enlighten them with the peaceful light of the good beginning, to allow the eyes of the heart to be illumined and your whole being to be converted by turning to the Lord with a love full of hope and open to everything new.

When the temptation to slow down the race or to come to a halt, when it insidiously installs itself in the spirit, it is good to go forth, turned toward our *beginning,* toward the roots which nourish the today of covenant with the Lord. A vital attitude for whoever wants to resist the demons of our weariness, who are able to paralyze us in the clutches of our hopelessness. The beginning is given. The source that fascinated us cannot deceive. God is attached to his creature with an indefectible manner. He loves us always and forever. His desire of communion with us makes him, the Poor One. He mercifully makes his way through our desertions, our resistances, our refusals to accord him love for love and to attach ourselves to him in tenderness and fidelity.

Without Shackles

To always remember her project helps us to advance with determination and courage on the evangelical road. Why fear, since God, who yesterday placed Clare and Agnes on the path, is still there today, closer than ever. They can follow the course with an unshakeable attachment to the God of the promise: *I am with you always; yes, to the end of time* (*Mt.* 28:20). Is this not dwelling in the human heart which houses the treasure of poverty? The certitude of this proximity allows Clare to write with assurance to Ermentrude: *Do not be afraid, daughter. God, Who is faithful in all His words and holy in all His deeds, will pour His blessings upon you and your sisters; and He will be your helper and the best consoler; He is our redeemer and our eternal reward* (*LEr* 15–16).

Thus, it is essential not to gather dust to weigh us down, but on the contrary, to leave behind all that would shackle the course. There is the fidelity to the call. Clare does not look back. The obstacles have not made her stumble. Uninterruptedly, she hopes, even if on certain days it is a challenge to rebuild her hope. Clare knows not only the dust, but also the harshness and the stones of the path. Prey to lack of understanding and to isolation, she must struggle with tenacity. But the trials do not cause her to withdraw into herself. On the contrary, the contradictions deepen her desire for a stronger and stronger attachment to the *Most-High*. Conscious of being called by the Spirit, she walks with the wisdom of the poor on the *path of happiness*.

Nothing disheartens her and it is in all truth that she writes in the heart of her *Form of Life*: *We had no fear of poverty, hard work, trial, shame, or contempt of the world, but, instead, we held them as great delights* (*RegCl* 6:2). And she confides to Brother Raynaldo: *After I once came to know the grace of my Lord Jesus Christ through his servant Francis, no pain has been bothersome, no penance too severe, no weakness, dearly beloved brother, has been hard* (*Cel* 44).

Run with Light Step

To enter into relationship with Clare is to enter into a race and to be carried by the momentum of a woman burning with love. What a paradox! The cloister of Saint Damian — restrained of itself — opens to the infinite: Clare, pilgrim of an interior adventure, always again places herself on the road toward her Lord. Her happiness? To chose to follow the same route as Jesus so as never to leave him. The loving kenosis of Christ captivates her and incites her to a Passover: a passage from a heavy and shackled step by a possessive self to a light race, brisk as a dance step, on the path of happiness. An astonishing exhortation of a sedentary to another sedentary!

By the most perfect poverty, writes her biographer, *she was eager to conform to the Poor Crucified, so that nothing transitory would separate the lover from the Beloved or would impede her way with the Lord (Cel* 14). Elsewhere, he notes with accuracy: *After leaving the world outside and enriching her mind within, she ran after Christ without being burdened with anything (Cel* 13). Clare encourages her friend to realize with determination and fidelity the proposal of life *in most high poverty.*

If the Son of God becomes the way, each instant offers the possibility of a new step that the stripping makes light. *Lady Poverty* espoused by Francis and Clare frees the heart in a race of which no obstacle can slow the momentum nor weigh down the step. She opens the road, narrow certainly, but most rapid and decisive. Clare knows neither indifference nor half-heartedness, even less sadness or discouragement.

It is the Spirit of the Lord who calls her and it is though *divine inspiration (RegCl* 2:1), that Clare and Agnes walk according to the way of the Son of God. From that time the path can only be blessed because God is the God of human happiness. His call does not make us dwarfed or grumpy, but upright and jubilant beings. Our race, far from being an apprehensive aspiration, becomes a confident relaxation and serene hope.

The *love of Christ overwhelms us,* says Saint Paul (2 Cor. 5:14). Clare can not put off today's step until tomorrow, neither can she stop on the road, because *at every hour, at every time of the day, every day and continually, let all of us truly and humbly believe, hold in our heart and love, honor, adore and serve the Lord God (1 Reg 23:11).*

Reflection Questions

Can you remember the starry hours of your life? Toward what have they oriented your path? Do you nourish this memory? How? When your steps become heavy, what enables you to find some lightness? How do the words, the life and the death of the Son of God enlighten your own road?

4
Contemplate the Morning

Focus Point

////////////

The race never stops except for those wonderful pauses in the presence of the surprising landscapes which leave us speechless before their beauty and their magnitude.

And such is the face of Jesus who offers Himself to us in the amazing humility and the touching poverty of a crib. Clare invites us to keep company with Him through a vigilant attention in searching for the discrete traces of His presence.

////////////

Christ is the radiance of eternal glory
He is the brightness of eternal light and the
mirror without blemish.
Gaze upon that mirror each day, O Queen
and Spouse of Jesus Christ,
and continually study your face in it,
that you may adorn yourself completely,

Within and without,
Covered and arrayed in needlework
and similarly adorned
  With the flowers and garments of all the virtues,
  as is becoming,
  the daughter and dearest bride of the Most
    High King.

Indeed, in that mirror,
  blessed poverty, holy humility, and inexpressible
    charity shine forth
  as with the grace of God,
you will be able to contemplate them throughout
  the entire mirror.
Look, I say, at the border of this mirror, that is,
  the poverty of Him
  Who was placed in a manger and wrapped in
    swaddling clothes.
  O marvelous humility!
  O astonishing poverty!
    The King of angels,
    The Lord of heaven and earth,
      Is laid in a manger!

          (4LAg 14–21)

Recognizing His Face

*C*lare's prayer is lived in the radiance of the Crucifix which spoke to Francis. During forty years, she contemplates him, icon of the Father, the face of his love without measure. This icon marks all of her spiritual experience with its unique traits. The extraordinary symbolic riches of the cross of Saint Damian exposes the whole history of salvation and the covenant of the *Most High* with humanity. This intimate covenant flashes forth from the love of the Crucified to the contemplative gaze of Clare and of her sisters. By her patient and loving contemplation, Clare interprets the vulnerability of God in the wounded and glorious body of Christ and in the heart of the *Father of Mercies.* Throughout her writing, the cross of Saint Damian projects its perplexing and blessed light. It reveals the solid and firm substructure of her prayer concentrated on a face — and a gaze fixed on this face — all the superabundant poverty of God surrendered to each one.

The crucified Beloved is the image of the Father and the reflection of a love never taken back. Clare leads us, very naturally, to stay with her before the spotless mirror of the eternal glory and the pure Love. The image of the mirror is borrowed from the Bible, which describes the divine Wisdom as *a reflection of the eternal light, an untarnished mirror of God's active power, and image of His goodness (Wis* 7:26). To clearly understand well the symbol of the mirror used by Clare, it is necessary to keep in mind the spirit of this text of Scripture. The mirror is Jesus, who at the same time, shows us who is God and reveals our unique beauty to us.

Clare invites her correspondent to pause for a long time before this mirror: *Gaze upon that mirror each day and continually study your face in it, contemplate, be attentive*....Thus, she will discover *herself*, clothed in the grace of the One she contemplates, clothed with the *"new person,"* *adorned with all the flowers and virtues* and of the dynamic strength of love.

From contemplation of Jesus, Clare receives the expression of the surprising splendor of God. It is truly in Him that God says to us. *There is no other Word, but him* (*Heb* 1:2), Jesus is the perfect Icon of the Father; anyone who *has seen me, has seen the Father* (*Jn* 14:9). The apostle Philip is heard to respond: In him, we know the visible face of God. At once, this face is contemplated by Clare as a luminous reality, beautiful and pure. Our hunger to know God finds some appeasement in the encounter that we daily receive in the face of the beloved Son of the Father.

Making allusion to the convex mirrors in three portraits, Clare perceives three high moments of his history in the life of Jesus: the morning of his birth, the day of his public life and the evening of his death. In her *Testament*, as she recalls her choice of poverty, she will exhort the sisters to remain faithful *out of love for the God Who was placed poor in the crib, lived poor in the world, and remained naked on the cross* (*TestCl* 45).

There, unfolds the geste of God in our history.

In the Poverty of the Crib

The dawn of the day of God begins in a crib!
God: a very tiny baby! *The King of the angels,
the Lord of heaven and earth, wrapped in swaddling
clothes*! Clare has the art of paradox, in a single
gaze, she embraces the whole mystery of the
kenosis of Jesus: *Who, being in the form of God, did
not count equality with God something to be grasped.
But he emptied himself, taking the form of a slave ...*
(*Ph* 2: 6–7). In his humility, God becomes a very
tiny baby. He accepts to be born in weakness, as
all other newborns, and in penury conditions
as a multitude of poor. At his birth, his unique
riches is the treasure of respect, of solicitude
and of tenderness of his mother who *envelopes
him in swaddling clothes.*

Clare insists and forcefully implores her sisters to be in deep communion with the poverty
of Jesus' beginnings! How? For example, in
their manner of dress: *Out of love of the most holy
and beloved Child wrapped in poor little swaddling
clothes and placed in a manger and of His most holy
Mother, I admonish, beg, and encourage my sisters
always to wear poor garments* (*RegCl* 2:24).

The actuality of the poverty of the Son of
God is not invisible to Clare. The poverty of
the crib does it shake our spiritual drowsiness
enough or have we popularized the crib and
the swaddling clothes of the "*little Jesus*" to the
point of no longer allowing our sensibility to

be touched, except momentarily, of such deri-
sory signs?

Welcome the Fragile Beginnings

Jesus' incarnation remains the way chosen
by God to tell us the value that we have in his
eyes and thus, to reveal to us our own grandeur. From the crib to the cross, the *Most High*
espouses our fragile humanity and rejoins it
beyond its incapacity to love.

The adventure of salvation begins in Mary's
body: *May you cling to His most sweet mother who
gave birth to a Son Whom the heavens could not
contain, and yet she carried Him in the little cloister
of her holy womb and held Him on her virginal lap*
(*3LAg* 18–19). The good fortune of poverty is
the first feature of the image that Clare contemplates in the mirror. It is that which appears, first
of all, and touches her gaze and her heart.

In Jesus, the poverty shines with a luminous
radiance. It receives from him its true sense,
unveiling the depths of its mystery. He comes to
us deprived and vulnerable to be able to reveal
its treasure. The true good, capable of leading
us to happiness, is hidden in the riches of the
relation to the Other and the others. It blossoms
in gratitude, in confident dependence and in
free self-effacement before Him. Our hesita-
tions, our wanderings and our failures can never
reduce us to deny the love that this poor God
came *so that you might become rich through his*

poverty (*2Cor* 8:9). The fragility of our uncertain steps contains the seed of a noted blessedness from the Lord and of which we grasp, through intermittence, some glittering:

> *O blessed poverty,*
> *who bestows eternal riches*
> *on those who love and embrace her.*

(1LAg 15)

Reflection Questions

Gazing on the crucifix of Saint Damian nourished the prayer of Clare. What are your sources where you quench your thirst for God? What is God's revelation to you in these sources? How can the birth of Jesus be inscribed in your daily life?

The image of a God who begs:

How does this shock you? How does it delight you? How can poverty enrich you?

5
Contemplate the Day

Focus Point

////////////

The dawn of salvation fills the day, our day.

It fills it with a humble and poor, ordinary and daily presence, which transfigures its heaviness. Difficult to tame a God who serves. Nevertheless, He is not elsewhere than where we are. The Very-Lowly washes our tired feet, taking on Himself "the innumerable fatigues and sufferings" of humanity.

////////////

> *Then reflect upon, at the surface of the mirror,*
> *the holy humility, at least the blessed poverty,*
> *the untold labors and punishments*
> *that He endured for the redemption of the*
> *whole human race.*

>   *(4LAg 22)*

////////////

Holy Humility

*I*n the Incarnation, blessed poverty is the faithful companion of the King of the angels. Never will she abandon him. In the public life of Jesus, it unfolds exteriorly as an existence without splendor which confines it in an unheard of anonymity. *His neighbors said of him: This is the carpenter, surely, the son of Mary, the brother of James and Joset and Jude and Simon? His sisters, too, are they not here with us? And they would not accept him (Mk 6:3).* God, could he always be elsewhere than there where we wait for him? Perhaps. If often we continue the search for his face under some magical forms, full of marvels, but empty of his true presence. Clare invites us to stop for a long time before the insignificance of a life marked by poverty, fatigues and sufferings. She understood with an extraordinary keenness that the highest spiritual realities are interpreted in the most ordinary. She never separates spiritual experience from the "domestic work"; there she discovers God in his humanity. She stretches the logic of the Incarnation until its ultimate consequences, the route of the poverty of Jesus: to travel the very banal narrow path of daily life as the only one by which she can rejoin him. The Word of God, spoken in love, withdraws and does not calculate its difficulty.

The Son of God lives "at ground level," if one dares to say, in the lowest of our human condition, allowing him to be wounded by our

difficulties and our sicknesses, to be touched by
our cries of distress and our cries for help. So
few are given to see! And the deception is not
distant, facing the existence of the *Most-High
Lord* so concealed in the humility of our days.
But his riches is to be with us: Emmanuel, present in the most obscure part of our history so as
to open there, the breakthrough of a new earth
and of new heavens. The God of the Holy of
Holies, the One before whom Moses took off his
sandals (*Ex* 3:5) and who enlightened the con-
science of Isaiah with his impurity (*Is* 6:5), walks
on our routes and is wounded by the brambles
and stones. His holiness slips completely into our
labors and our pains in order to transfigure and
make them light by his presence. *Come to me, all
you who labor and are overburdened, and I will give
you rest* (*Mt* 11:28). Our prayer, will it cleanse our
gaze to discover, even in the most lifeless hours,
the luminous shadow of a God of humility?

God Serving

In chapter 13 of his Gospel, the Apostle John
retraces for us the event of the washing of the
feet. He defines the passage of Jesus toward his
Father as the fullness of love toward the Father
and others. *Having loved those who were his in the
world, He loved them to the end* (*Jn* 13:1). The hour
has come for Jesus to reveal to us how much
God is love. He tells us, not in a discourse, but
in a simple gesture, inscribes *in the most ordinary*

existence, a gesture which recreates, restores and rehabilitates. Jesus *got up from table, removed his outer garments and, taking a towel wrapped it round his waist; he then poured water into a basin and began to wash the disciples' feet and to wipe them with the towel he was wearing (Jn* 13: 4–5). There is the unparalleled God whom Jesus reveals: God very small at the feet of the man and woman of whom he acknowledges all their grandeur! God on his knees in front of us! God ties his apron each time that man or woman needs to be served, to have their feet washed, relieved of the dust of their battles, of their struggles and of their labors. We fully understand the strong reaction of Peter! As him, we bristle up: *Never! You shall never wash my feet. If I do not wash you, you can have no share with me (Jn* 13:8). The response of Jesus sends us back to the desire underneath our prayer: *to be with him,* to have part in all that which he is and engage ourselves in the same way of stripping and of surrendered love. Here is the path of our salvation.

With much theological finesse, Clare affirms that not only the three days of the passion, death and resurrection are the source of salvation for the world, but also the hidden life at Nazareth and the public life. In each gesture and in each encounter or word of Jesus, all the love of the Father is engaged and offered. He is of the same reality of our life, whether it be harsh or luminous. God finds his joy in keeping us on our feet and by indefatigably sharing with us his faithful love and the value that we have in his eyes. *I have given you an example so that you may copy what I have done to you.... Now that you know this, blessed are you if you behave accordingly* (*Jn* 13: 15–17). For Clare, *mother and servant of the Poor Sisters of Saint Damian* (*TestCl* 79), there does not exist any other key to happiness than to love as the Son of God by following the path of the Lord. It is there that the Master and Lord encounters you for a *joy no one shall take from you* (*Jn* 16:22).

The Day of God in our Days

The washing of the feet represents, for Francis and Clare, the fundamental gesture of the poor Lord. Contemplate it, listen to it and make it your own is wisdom for the poor one who desires *to embrace the poor Christ* (*2LAg* 18). The poor Christ, Clare said to us, is the unique mirror infinitely faithful to the likeness of God. One understands the invitation of Clare to gaze on this mirror each day. We cannot know Love without it being our dwelling by an assiduous prayer in the mystery of the poverty of the Lord. *Each day*, she says to us ... neither in a distracted manner, nonchalant, nor without taking time to place in our heart, and even in our body, the weight of such humility understood only by the human spirit. Now, this incredible revelation, according to Clare, is not contemplated in a divine elsewhere, far from our familiar hori-

zons. *The blessedness of poverty* is inscribed in the
monotony of our days! In the heart of our tasks
often banal and routine, in the time that escapes
us, the sweetness of the time of God flows out,
full of confidence, of courage and of serenity.
The life and its complexity can very often discourage us. The certitude, even fragile, of the
divine presence prevents us from losing heart.
When the months and the years weaken our
strengths, erode the sense of the things to do, of
objectives to follow, and it is necessary to come
to the end of our choices; the joy of commun-
ing with Jesus, there where we are and in what
we are living, suffices to bring peace and savor
to our existence. When boredom makes taste-
less our fervor, we know where to find God. In
the *countless fatigues and sufferings,* the love of the
poor Christ draws us toward the blessedness of
the Father who does not want anything to keep
us from Him and who gives everything to the
one who wholeheartedly receives it.

Reflection Questions

   "Would God always be elsewhere rather
than there where we await Him?" When you
affirm: "God was there." Why this assurance?
To what do your connect His presence? Why
this self-effacement of God? How can you
receive your existence as the experience of a
loving encounter with God?

6
Contemplate the Evening

Focus Point

Poverty and solitude do not extinguish the dawn.
The cry of thirst which escapes from Jesus' lips on the cross is the cry of a God who passionately loves His creature. God asks us, in this cry, to refresh His heart, to alleviate His thirst and to join Him in His pain. It is so only that the fruits of happiness, health and life are born on the tree of love without measure.

Finally contemplate, in the depth of this same mirror,
the ineffable charity that He chose to suffer on the tree of the Cross
and to die there the most shameful kind of death.

Therefore,
that mirror, suspended on the wood of the Cross,

> warned those passing by that here are things to
>   be considered, saying:
>   All you who pass by the way,
>   look and see if there is any suffering like
>   my suffering.
>   Let us respond to Him,
>   Crying out and lamenting, in one voice, in one
>   spirit:
>   Remembering this over and over
>   leaves my soul sinking within me.
>   (4LAg 23–26)

////////////

He Remained Naked on the Tree

*T*he poverty and humility of Christ con-templated by Clare are the most delicious fruits of love. Furthermore, they are its other names. They flow out from it as a gentle strength and renew it. For Jesus, the path of love "until the end" blossoms on the cross.

In contemplating Christ crucified, Clare remains before the burning bush in a totally free gift of herself, pure offering and radical gift. If the love of God is revealed by the whole life of Jesus, no part is more resplendent with such brightness as the hour where he accepts to die the *most shameful death.* In this hour, Jesus is poor in the most high poverty, reviled in his nakedness, rejected by all and betrayed by his close friends. Already the *swaddling clothes* of the newborn of

Bethlehem are lamentable, but at least, they speak of the tenderness and the respect of a mother. On Calvary, Jesus is exposed naked to the sneering of the crowd. The poor man of Nazareth becomes a *poor man* delivered to derision and shame. At Golgotha, the contempt and the incomprehension attain their climax. Humanity's rejection of the love offered by the Crucified inscribes the sharpest wounds in the heart of the Father.

Love is not loved! Francis would have wanted to roam the earth weeping for the Passion of the Lord. He communed without limit in every fibre of his being to this love of the Son of God; so much that the marks of the Passion of the *poor Crucified* were imprinted in his flesh. For Clare, no stigmata. Nevertheless, how can we believe that a woman, also passionate toward her Lord nailed on a cross *by love of our love,* did not carry in her being the most profound wound of such offering?

God Thirsts

Until now, Clare asks us to gaze. And here, she invites us to enter in dialogue. Brusquely, the *mirror placed on the wood of the cross* comes to life. A moan is raised in the middle of the silence. From the mouth of Jesus on the cross, Clare receives a lamentation of a humiliated Jerusalem, *Look and see: is any sorrow like the sorrow inflicted on me* (*Lam* 1:12). Sorrow that Saint John will translate as a last cry: *I am thirsty* (*Jn* 19:28). On the cross, Jesus knows an unfathomable solitude. The solitude of a surrendered love only encounters the silence of escape, incomprehension and refusal. Jesus' dying cry unveils his infinite desire and his thirst of communion with the creature. He wounds the heart of Clare, allowing her to accept insofar as she is able his *inexpressible love.*

The prayer before the Crucified is an exchange. The charity of the Son of God, during the hour of the Passion and death, is not a reality which we can contemplate while remaining exterior to the drama without taking the risk of simply being engaged there as actors. The prayer of Clare and in following her, our own, becomes an encounter, a dialogue of love and compassion, a listening to be able to understand through the grace of the Spirit and the incomprehensible disproportion of the mercy of the Father. This contemplation is inscribed in the memory: *I could not ever forget it.* Jesus' Passion lives day and night in Clare. The suffering of the Beloved becomes one's own in a communion that is at the same time suffering and wonderment. Here is a prayer which she confides to Ermentrude of Bruges when she writes to her: *From the depths of your being, love God and Jesus, His Son, Who was crucified for us sinners, and never let the thought of Him leave your mind. Meditate constantly on the mysteries of the cross and the agonies of His mother standing at the foot of the cross* (*LEr* 11–12).

May I Die for Love of Your Love

So often our prayer is filled with what we want to say to God. And there on the cross, he implores us, he seeks to have us take heed of his sorrow and to have compassion for his unjust suffering. Christ is made a beggar of love from each of us. His invitation to gaze upon his sorrow, wounds the heart of Clare. She becomes vulnerable to the image of the poor Crucified. *This memory consumes me....* With Clare, we can remain in a distressed tenderness, as poor as it might be, which will unite us to the Beloved, becoming a silent and loving presence, suffering with his suffering and not leaving Christ alone in the moment of the height of distress. A long and difficult apprenticeship for the one who consents to be ill from that which wounds him and to allow the pain of God to touch us, affect us and become our own.

Costly in Yahweh's sight is the death of his faithful (*Ps* 115: 15) says the Psalmist. Each human being is a beloved child of God. In his Father's heart, the suffering is, also, inordinate even if only one of his little ones doesn't know the beatitude. Jesus, poor and crucified, Clare contemplates him and comes to his aid *in each of the weak members of His ineffable Body* (*3LAg* 8). In her compassion, she remembers the Passion of Christ and perceives it reflected in every suffering reality. Thus, Clare rejoins the women of the Gospel, and standing at the foot of the cross, her vigilant love offers a resting place to God's sorrow.

The Fruits of the Cross

Clare does not observe at a distance the salvific strength of the Crucified, but she allows herself to be totally enveloped by it. Immediately, by grace she becomes a source of salvation and of health for her suffering brothers and sisters. In prayer, she participates in the love of the Crucified who heals: little by little, the *indescribable love* of God is imprinted in her heart, a marvelous exchange in which she gathers, from the tree of the cross, all the strength of a benevolent and good life that love communicates. *The beloved Crucified took possession of the lover, and she was inflamed with such love of the mystery of the Cross that the power of the Cross is shown by signs and miracles. In fact, when she traced the sign of the life-giving Cross on the sick, sickness miraculously fled from them* (*Cel* 32). Her thoughtful attention prompts her to relieve her sisters and the sick as much as she is able. *With all the strength of her faith,* she offers herself in the destitute so that through her, the Crucified can continue his work. Not with magic, but in blessing each of her sisters, Clare, little and poor, offers the free space where she will be able to open out in grace, thus, manifesting that God alone is the source of all good.

To consider the mystery of the *ineffable charity* of God in Christ on the Cross guides us to the same fecundity because love is given to be poured out: *become the one whom you contemplate.*

Reflection Questions

Have you experienced abandonment, loneliness, even rejection or treason? What were the fruits of these events in life? In practice, does the cry of Jesus on the Cross touch you? Can you bring healing there? What response do you give him? Which acts give him an echo in your life today and in the world?

7
Desire Jesus

Focus Point

////////////

The loving gaze posed on Jesus nourishes the strong desire in Clare to always remain with Him. In her frantic race to join Him, she begs Him never to leave her. The perfume of His poverty draws her into the "cellar," a place of intimacy and of loving inebriation.

There we could be tempted to abandon our race with a beautiful precursor. "Too big," "too beautiful," "such momentum is not for us!" But Clare says to us with her whole being that we are promised the same happiness, and that holiness is simply "to be hungry for God."

////////////

O Queen of our heavenly King, may you, there-fore, be inflamed ever more strongly with the fire of love! As you further contemplate His ineffable delights, riches and perpetual honors, and, sighing,

*may you cry out from the great desire and love of
your heart:*

*Draw me after you, let us run in the fragrance of
your perfumes, O heavenly Spouse!*

*I will run and not tire, until you bring me into the
wine cellar,*

*Until your left hand is under my head and your
right hand will embrace me happily,*

*You will kiss me with the happiest kiss of your
mouth.*

(4LAg 27–32)

*T*hese last days, Clare guided us before
a mirror: the Son of God, poor and
crucified. She invited us to gaze on Him, to
contemplate Him and to look at ourselves there
each day. The contemplation of the newborn of
Bethlehem, of the poor man of Nazareth and of
the Crucified hollows out in her a desire ablaze
with the fire of the love of God. Prayer is not
pure passivity; it becomes enamored of the same
Love and wants to identify with him. Pilgrim
and stranger, Clare does not want to live for herself alone, but for Christ and to allow Him to
dwell in her. *Never desire anything except to unite
yourself to the poor and crucified Christ* (*1LAg* 13).

The morning, the day and the evening of the
most beautiful of the children of men awakens in
her an ardent and strong love which she herself
wanted in the proportion of the disproportion

of the divine charity. This is not a powerless silence, sorrowful and grieved which responds to the Crucified, but the passionate cry *of all love* which wants to be totally in intimate conversation with the Beloved, without ever to be separated from him. Clare knew the pain of thirst that nothing satisfies: *Very frequently, while she was prostrate on her face in prayer, she flooded the ground with tears and caressed it with kisses, so that she might always seem to have her Jesus in her hands, on whose feet her tears flowed and her kisses were impressed* (*Cel* 19).

Draw Me

Likewise, God's Word provides Clare with the words of her prayer, *Draw me in your footsteps, let us run* (*Ct* 1:4). In the Middle-Ages, the monks borrowed from the *Canticle of Canticles* the loving vocabulary of the Beloved to express the sorrow of the search for God, the emptiness of His absence or the beatitude and the sweetness of His presence. This book very rapidly became the hidden treasure where the searchers of God draw the words to express their passionate love.

The life of every baptized person is to be plunged into the intimacy of God and in the mystery of his love. *The Canticle of Canticles* touches each one of us in the most profound intimacy of our relationship with him. It tells the beauty of the communion of love to which we are henceforth invited. It opens the singular space for our desire to travel and the vastness to pass-over in every sense and in all of the senses, so as to live in the secret garden.

Draw me.... Clare is not yet in the palace of the *King of Heaven.* She is always in exile in the cloister of Saint Damian, given over to her fragility. Her call is a supplication of which she is unable to do anything by herself, but dares all in the strength of her Beloved. Love's pressing demand to Love. Is this not *the fire of love* which implores Christ to make her step swift and joyful on the path to union?

The *perfume* places Clare in movement, going forth to follow it. As the wind spreads the perfume of the flowers and fruits around, thus the Spirit blows the perfume of Christ, a trace of His presence in His absence, toward Clare. Marveling at the gift given to her, Clare suggests to Agnes, as well as to each one of us to not hold back, but to breathe the perfume of the *poverty of the Lord Jesus Christ: be very joyful and glad, filled with a remarkable happiness and a spiritual joy* (1LAg 21).

As Far as the Wine Cellar

The poor lady of Saint Damian does not stop her race in the following of the poor Jesus before reaching her goal. In her determination, nothing can weaken her. *I will run and not tire....* Love frees her from herself and makes her supple. In the grace of Christ, the strength of her desire draws her more and more toward the Spouse.

In the *Canticle of Canticles*, the wine cellar represents the place of intimacy of the bride and the groom, where the encounter blossoms in the embrace. Distance and absence are abolished. Upheld by the spouse, the beloved no longer fears anything because she finds herself in the same secure place as in the plenitude. There, Clare abandons herself to the tenderness of the *poor Crucified.*

With the happiest kiss of their mouth, the bride and the groom share the same breath, participate in the same life and commune with the same will. Clare tastes a new happiness. All her history and her person are marked from the imprint of the *poor Crucified,* which acknowledges in her life the icon of his own abasement, molded by humility, poverty and simplicity.

Henceforth, she can lead and encourage her sisters into an uncertain future by exhorting them to have the utmost confidence. The wine cellar of the most intimate union with the Lord is hidden not in the heights of a prayer disengaged from reality, but in the "lowest" of difficulties, fragility, powerlessness and abandonment into his hands day after day. The simple step, which thrusts one deeper into Gospel poverty, already filled Clare. It strengthens her courage and opens even more her desire to become totally one with Christ in the fullness of the Kingdom.

The Mystique, a Shared Love

The writings of Clare — or of other saints — can appear as some very fastidious garments much too large for us. It is necessary to resist the temptation to reduce them to our size and thus run the risk of having skimpy garments so that we cannot move with ease and freedom. Contrary to what we could believe, we can enter in their spiritual approach. The mystical life does not consist of exceptional phenomena, but in a life of faith inflated with love and hope. It is simply the unfolding in us of the baptismal grace by which each one of us is called to communion with God in Jesus Christ.

Certainly, we have not yet been able to integrate in our own spiritual growth such personal experience. But to gaze, to love and to pray with Clare of Assisi allows us to understand how contemplation is not the privilege of those who can offer themselves to leisure and luxury of a silent environment while isolating themselves momentarily from their daily preoccupations. Our desire of Jesus is not to be measured by our spiritual comfort or personal harmony. Clare contemplates an Image, not to study abstractly the outlines, but to allow herself to be transformed by him. The mystical life is neither moral life nor an ascetic route, it is a shared passion. Our dullness of spirit, our failures as well as our wanderings are not obstacles to our encounter with the Beloved. If, in the daily compost where we live, we hear the desire of Jesus rise in our heart and respond to him in the simplicity of faith, we discover, little by little, the good fortune of the poor whom he fills with his riches.

Reflection Questions

Contemplation of the Poor Crucified awakens Clare's love. Couldn't it also awaken other feelings? Are you interested in this intimacy with God? How could it be expressed in your life? If the mystical life is "shared passion" where do we find its traces? If holiness is a hunger of God, how can we appease this hunger?

8
Receive Some Persons to Love

Focus Point

////////////////

The intimacy of the embrace is as vast as love.
Names jostle each other and we offer them the
hospitality of a faithful and strong friendship.
There is nothing to fear in loving, immersed in the
source of love. It is with the same heart that we
are stirred in the name of the beloved Lord Jesus
and with the names of those who hold our gaze;
ask for our tenderness and offer us their affection.
God created us in His image and likeness. In a
moving dialogue of love, our human friendships
are the words with which He disposes for us to be
able to breathe with his own breath.

////////////////

Resting in this contemplation, may you
remember your poor little mother, knowing
that I have inscribed the happy memory of

*you indelibly on the tablets of my heart,
holding you dearer than all others.*

*What more? In your love may the tongue of
the flesh be silent; may the tongue of the Spirit
speak and say this: O blessed daughter, because
the love that I have for you can never be fully
expressed by the tongue of the flesh, it says,
what I have written is inadequate. I beg you to
receive my words with kindness and devotion,
seeing in them at least the motherly affection
that in the fire of charity I daily feel toward
you and your daughters to whom I warmly
commend myself and my daughters in Christ.*

*On their part, these daughters of mine,
especially the most prudent virgin Agnes, our
sister, recommend themselves in the Lord to
you and your daughters as much as they can.*

*Farewell, my dearest daughter, with your
daughters until we meet at the throne of the
glory of the great God and desire [this] for us.*
                                   (4LAg 33–39)

//////////////

*T*his text concludes the *Fourth letter to Agnes
of Prague* on which we have meditated
these last four days. Entering with Clare and Agnes
into the contemplation of Jesus, Icon of poverty,
of humility and of love of the Father, we can be
surprised at this sudden call to allow the tenderness
which lives in us to awaken regarding our friends.

Open Space of the Embrace

The door of the wine cellar, far from enclos-
ing us in the embrace, allows the affective
potential of the beloved to blossom exteriorly.
For Clare, the love of Jesus, poor and humble,
does not narrow the heart in a withdrawal
where she alone tastes the beauty and goodness
of the Lord. The *embrace* does not close her
within herself in a protected spiritual universe.
Therefore, her contemplation has nothing of a
solitary heart to heart.

With a marvelous audacity and a touching
spontaneity, Clare inserts in the treasure chest
of her communion with the Beloved, all those
whom she loves with a preferential love. She
cannot incur the reproach of making her most
elevated prayer as a refuge for her and her God.
To search a shelter in prayer without bringing
the network of relationships into that which we
live, is not what we have learned in the teaching
of Jesus. Can we offer the most beautiful hospitality of our prayer to our friends? Led by Clare
on a covenant path, we discover a love which
gives and shares, the source and the truth of our
human tenderness.

The Christ encountered in contemplation is
never alone. Always he comes to us as the path to
the Father and to others. His gaze, before whom
Clare prays, is never only on her, it is focused
on a thousand faces. Jesus of Nazareth is eter-

nal gaze, within which, each one becomes precious, unique and beloved. No doubt the Lord
addresses to her the same prayer as to Mary
Magdalene on Easter morning: *Do not cling to
me … go and find my brothers* (*Jn* 20:17). For her,
to commune with her Beloved, it is to commune
with the same ardent love with those who share
in her heart and her life. *The fire of love* with
which she is embraced by the poor Crucified
equally inflames her — totally — with regard to
Agnes and her sisters. As the little garden of San
Damiano opens out on the vast plains of Assisi,
her heart is enlarged in the infinite dimensions
of the heart of God.

Some Persons to Love

Clare received from Jesus the riches of her
affectivity. And all her friendships become
inseparable from this first and foundational
love: *The love of God has been poured forth in our
hearts by the Holy Spirit who has been given to us*
(*Rm* 5:5). One and the same affective strength
is given to us to love the Lord Jesus and to love
our neighbors. In this unique love, we love
the One and the others. Without a doubt, for
Clare, intimate union with her *Spouse, who is in
the heavens*, transforms into a burning bush of
inexpressible love of God in which her *maternal
affection* and her preferential love with regard to
Agnes and her sisters, unfolds all her potenti-

alities! The good tree of contemplation carries
in itself the enjoyable fruit of friendship....

God is relationship. The spiritual life consists
in allowing oneself to be in relationship with him,
with our brothers and sisters and with the universe
itself. Of the same momentum, Clare goes to God
and to others with all her feminine sensibility and
vibrant affection without disavowing any of her
capacity to love with tenderness. Her joy of being
a Poor Sister radiates in each one of her relationships and authenticates them because it is only
happiness that offers, welcomes and shares. In the
heart of prayer, to *remember* Jesus and to *remember*
someone or what one loves, leads to the same and
unique beatitude.

Hymn to Friendship

Very naturally, her song of love toward
the Beloved, blossoms in the happiness of the
embrace and gives birth to a touching hymn of
friendship. Clare measures the powerlessness
of words to stammer out the treasure of love
which burns her. Desolate of not being able
to adequately translate it, she wishes to allow
the tongue of the Spirit to speak in her. Only
the "love of God poured out in our hearts" can
spell out the friendship, which within his infinite
riches, he gives us to share through our awk-
ward gestures and words. In *engraving forever on
the tablets of our heart* the beloved names, Clare
participates in truth to the faithful tenderness of

the One who has imprinted our names on the palm of his hands (*Is* 49:16).

The love that she feels for her friend is named *dilection.* There is the fruit which God's friendship matured in her. This word is rich with a triple signification which gives to each relationship its unique coloration. Above all, friendship appears as a "reading" of the other and a "harvest" of all that it is in truth. This welcome leads to a choice, that is to say, a wonder and an attachment where tenderness and respect is encouraged. In the ultimate choice, the loved person is finally preferred and chosen from among all the others. This love of *dilection* places its seal on every fiber of our being. It establishes a constant communion which knows neither lukewarmness nor indifference. Prayer cannot make us insensible beings. The love of friendship is never disincarnate. On the contrary, the encounter with Jesus refines our capacity to love, purifies our sensibility and further humanizes us. Finally, Clare can display all her feminine tenderness according to multiple overtones: *spouse, sister, mother, daughter....* In its totality, the relational register cannot exhaust any of the intensity and the riches of her sentiments: this affection never comes from her and she does not search to grasp this gift.

The fire of love, and the happiness which flows from it, celebrates friendship as a sacrament of the Invisible. In our human affections, we interpret the limpid parable, likewise, of God, because *God is friendship* (*Aelred of Rievaulx*).

Reflection Questions

The place of intimacy is an open space. How to live prayer which is not "just you and God," close and comfortable, but a hospitality which is offered to your family, your close relations, and your friends and to all humanity? How can prayer send you on mission or be an incentive to go elsewhere? It is impossible to separate Jesus from this world which He loves. How, then, can I love this world when it, sometimes, appears not very "lovable"? If I have only one heart with which to love, how can I unify this heart, and in Him, all our loves?

9
Allow Yourself to Be Transformed

Focus Point

////////////

In this ninth step Clare teaches us how we can continue the road, now transformed in the image of the One who never leaves us. To gather us within His gaze, with a pacified spirit and a happy heart, is a vast program in our agitated existences. This exchange of glances fans in us the flame of the outpouring of love who *gives Himself totally to us.* Thus, His sweetness, a new savor, flows throughout our entire being.

////////////

Who is there, then, who would not encourage me to rejoice over such marvelous joys? Therefore, dearly beloved, may you too always rejoice in the Lord. And may neither bitterness nor a cloud overwhelm you,

*O dearly beloved Lady in Christ, joy of the
angels and crown of your sisters!*

(3LAg 9–14)

///////////////

Clare does not lead us to inaccessible heights.
In the mirror which she daily contemplates, we
can reflect on ourselves because Jesus is within
each of us, day after day. How can we experience the same peace and enjoy an intimacy
similar to this which Clare knew? In this ninth
day of our journey in prayer, Clare traces us a
very simple itinerary, possible for everyone, in
order that in our turn we are able to become the
one we contemplate and reunite in our prayer.

Resist Moroseness

A first step which is proposed to us: resist
bitterness. Why allow the air of our heart to
be polluted by the dust of our vexations in our
limits and the parasites of our frustrations?
We could risk overshadowing the divine image
which is little by little being restored in us. May
the merciful patience on the part of the Lord
clarify whatever alters its beauty....

To which remedy can we run to dissipate
the fog which renders us insensible to the sun
of love? *Always be joyful*, responds Clare. The
joy of the poor heart is not less real than the
greediness of life. It is nourished by an interior
attitude of deeper and deeper dispossession of

self which neither leaves a place for bitterness nor for deception nor withdrawal of self. Light joy, discreet joy and interior lightness so as to cast aside the weight of things and of oneself in order to embrace Jesus, *the treasure hidden in the field of the world.*

With Your Whole Being

To contemplate Jesus does not suppose that we leave aside a part of ourselves outside of our spiritual adventure. *Intelligence, breath and heart* are equally affected by the desire to see God and to welcome his love.

In this second step, we are only asked to reassemble our being so often dispersed and to allow it, little by little, to be unified under the gaze of Jesus. How? Clare says: *Place yourself...,* Take the time to sit down, to stop to rest. Nothing else! The supreme activity of such an attitude is in appearance the most passive. Certainly, the preceding days, Clare has suggested for us to turn toward Christ, the mirror of the Father. To follow the poor Christ, she presses us to let go of everything: the esteem, the image that we have of ourselves. In this new step of prayer, it is a question of allowing us to be totally *transformed in the image of God: place your intelligence, your breath, your heart....* Prayer places us entirely in the mystery of the humility of the Son of God and converts us into a mirror of the poverty of the Father.

Marvelous Exchange

Flee the moroseness engendered in every form of self-centeredness and "place" yourself before Jesus, image of the Father, in self-forgetfulness and lack of mastery of yourself. There are the two steps suggested by Clare to enter in a *marvelous exchange* and to know the *sweetness of God*.

Exchange of gazes which turn our lives upside down: progressively, we become that upon which we gaze. A part of the mystery of the other dwells in us and becomes ours through our reception of it. At the same time, our gaze leads us back to the truest depths of the mystery of our person. *Something passes between us,* we say familiarly. The space which delineates the exchange of gazes can appear uninhabited. It is, in effect, but in the manner of a path which bonds again two dwellings. Respect, sweetness and wonder inhabit it and establish it in the course of the journey as a mysterious communion of souls. It is the same when we keep ourselves before Jesus. In the transforming strength born of love, we are recreated and we are reborn to our true being. Icon of the Father, Jesus transfigures us into this same icon. The slow work of grace most often eludes our consciousness, as the result is still imperfect but not less real. *Mirror of the Invisible, Resplendent of Glory*, Jesus allows us to participate in the beauty of God. From him, we receive our original grace. This transfiguration is not the fruit of an exterior imitation, but the outpouring of the love of God in our life.

Her memory continually pictured Him Whom love had profoundly impressed upon her heart (*Cel* 30). Thus, all the grandeur and the dignity of our own heart is revealed: *Indeed, it is now clear that the soul of a faithful person, the most worthy of all creatures because of the grace of God, is greater than heaven itself, since the heavens and the rest of creation cannot contain their Creator; only a faithful soul is His dwelling place and throne, and this only through the charity that the wicked lack* (*3LAg* 21–22). God is "more intimate to us than we ourselves": we carry in us the Creator of the heavens. Since the Incarnation, the Holy of Holies is no longer in the Temple, but in our fragile humanity where our love, preceded by that of our Creator, is aroused, vivified and nourished. There, God himself comes to open out our capacity to love. Far from being a theological abstraction, "the divine inhabitation" is really the presence of the poor God in us. He chooses us to become as Mary, *His Palace, His Tabernacle, His Dwelling* (*SalBVM* 4). In the simplicity and humility of our lives, He finds *my home* (*Ps* 131:14). What other reason can we give for our own unique grandeur and of the sacred dignity of each human person?

Savor the Secret Sweetness

The insistence of Clare to place our whole being *in the mirror of the life without end* does not only lead us to transform ourselves to the point of being able to say with Saint Paul: *It is no longer I, but Christ living in me* (*Gal* 2:20). To dwell in him, also allows us *to savor the sweetness of God*. Mystical excess? Far from it. *God is extraordinary sweetness*, sings Francis. This sweetness, antidote to the bitterness of certain realities in our life, is a trace of God in us. The "taste" of God and of his mystery is sweetness for whoever, in faith, allows oneself to be progressively grasped by him to every level of one's being. We enjoy the respect of a Lord, himself poor, who does not impose himself on the loved one. The fruit of the communion with Jesus crucified takes the savor of a reciprocal gift. *May you totally love Him Who gave Himself totally for your love* (*3LAg* 15). God touches to liberate. He calls us to become like him by transforming us into the Image of his divinity.

Reflection Questions

Clare's counsels are rare. Those of this ninth day are invaluable and concrete. Will you choose joy and resist moroseness, today? Will you take this invaluable time of a gratuitous emptiness "to recollect yourself" today under the loving glance of God? If "God is more intimate to us than we are to ourselves," where do we look to encounter Him and to contemplate Him?

How can prayer change you?

10
Become Listening

///////////////

This proximity, this dwelling of God in us will pro-
duce various and tasty fruits. To listen and receive
the Word nourishes this communion with the
Beloved. The awkwardness of the language of the
preacher, the roughness of the bark, nothing is able
to divert the spirit and the heart of Clare from the
Word which she masticates with respect and happiness, such good bread indispensable to her life.

///////////////

*Clare provided for her children, through
dedicated preachers, the nourishment of
the Word of God and from this she did not
take a poorer portion. She was filled with
such rejoicing at hearing a holy sermon; she
delighted at such a remembrance of her Jesus
… Although she was not educated in the*

liberal arts, she nevertheless enjoyed listening to the sermons of those who were because she believed that a nucleus lay hidden in the text that she would subtly perceive and enjoy with relish. She knew what to take out of the sermon of any preacher that might be profitable to the soul, while knowing that to pluck a flower from a wild thorn was no less prudent than to eat the fruit of a noble tree.

(Cel 37)

*I*n the course of the years, with the patience of time and persevering prayer, Jesus becomes closer to us and more familiar. Progressively, we become familiar with the traits of his face. Contemplation carries its fruit. It renders us, little by little, similar to him by participating in the same breath. It makes ours, his words and his actions. The Spirit who loved Jesus of Nazareth reposes on us. He inspires us as he has inspired Clare, Francis and so many others. He creates a desire in us to enter into the sentiments of Christ, to love those whom he loves and to suffer with those who suffer. At the mercy of our docility to his action, he imprints in our lives the ways of God such as Scripture reveals them to us.

Bonded through fraternal love, Clare and her sisters lived this interior transformation in a poor and humble existence. Where can they draw a true and sweet knowledge of Christ, if not by listening to the Word?

A Heart that Listens

God is the God of the Word. Such a mirror, the Word reveals us to ourselves. It brings us to our deepest self. In it, we can know our heart and enter into a dialogue, often stammering but always responsible, with the God who becomes near: *The Word is very near to you; it is in your mouth and in your heart for you to put into practice* (*Dt* 30:14). The Word of the Book heard during the liturgy and meditated in silence is slowly imprinted in us. It speaks to us of God and explains the long history of the Covenant which he forms with each one as well as with his people. It deciphers our own holy history with us and discovers therein the desire of God. To hear it, it is necessary for us to let go of our make-believe and of all that blocks a simple welcome of the presence of the poor and vulnerable God. Poverty and silence of the heart hollow out an opening and an availability to allow us to be surprised by him. Loving, the prayer is first of all, attentive listening of the other, of this Other, the Beloved of the Father (*Mk* 9:7).

If our eyes plunge in the mirror to contemplate *the resplendence of the glory of God*, our ears are opened wide to penetrate the music of the human language by which God chooses to speak to us. This patient assimilation of the Word *completely transforms your entire being into the image of the Godhead Itself, so that you too may feel what friends feel in tasting the hidden sweetness* (*3LAg* 13–14).

The Almond in the Shell

Lady Clare took pleasure to hear the Word of God, declared Sister Agnes in the *Process of Canonization*. The preaching and the liturgy offer itself to her as the privileged places through which she reaches him. Despite the poverty of the means of exegetical knowledge of her time, Clare gives proof of an astonishing familiarity with the Bible. Her writings are impregnated with it. Neither the roughness of the biblical language nor its enigmas discourage her heart, so avid to know the Beloved. Even the limits of the discourse of the preachers cannot block her pressing desire *to learn something new from the Lord* (*Cel* 45). All light, all intelligence that she receives in sharing, encounters in her a humble and joyful welcome. She marvels of God who, in the deviation of our human words, surprises her with a flash of his mystery. No sermon, even mediocre, disheartens her. The delicateness of her love awakened her and permitted her *to gather a flower on a thorn bush*! Free of all prejudgment before the fervent preachers who transmitted to her the Word, she is only pure and simple listening for the treasure buried in field of the Scriptures. *She knows that the almond is hidden under the appearance of the words; she appreciates it with finesse and savors it with delight.*

Clare masticates the Word as one masticates with respect and happiness the bread which makes us live. Without respite, her loving quest breaks through the exterior meaning of the words of the Book, the matrix of human discourse, as she decodes the hidden mystery in the most banal and daily reality of her community. She wants to reach the almond, the savory fruit of the Presence, who delivers himself, *nourishment of life* for her pilgrimage, bread of the heart which fortifies the sisters of San Damiano more than the bread begged for the body. What joy to drill unceasingly in the well of the Word in order to drink water, always new, and to quench one's thirst, day after day, in the living memory of the One who has seduced her, Jesus, the poor *Crucified*. Her listening welcomes this God who never imposes himself, but who comes to us under the most humble guise of the human word. Without hesitation, her faith recognized the footprints of the unique Word of the *One who ruled and still rules heaven and earth* (*1LAg* 17).

What happiness for this passionate woman to hear the brothers of Francis comment on the Word and preach to the Sisters! As Marie at the feet of Jesus (*Lk* 10: 38–42), avid to inscribe on *the tablets of her heart*, the traces of the beloved face and his vivifying words, *she takes for herself the better part of the spiritual nourishment.* What one biographer says to us about Francis applies perfectly to Clare: *He sometimes read the Sacred Books, and whatever he once put into his mind, he wrote indelibly in his heart. His memory took the place of books, Because, if he heard something once, it was not wasted, as his heart would mull it over with constant devotion* (*2Cel* 102).

Let us place ourselves in the school of Clare and of Francis. Let us open our ears each morning for the Word, always fresh from God who wants to make all things new in our lives (*Rev* 21:5). May the One who is called the Way instruct us and of whom the voice, in a roundabout way of each page of the Scripture, invites us to be nourished by his word of love: *I shall instruct you and teach you the way to go; I shall not take my eyes off you* (*Ps* 31:8).

The discrete word of the Lord is hidden under the exterior of the text of the biblical Books, of the commentaries and other means placed at our disposition to foster our understanding and our meditation of the texts. But in the following of Clare, it is necessary for us to venture beyond. Within the text, broken by our loving listening, welcome the Lord who gives himself. Beyond the noise of the words and of the discourse, the personal communion with the Son of God is a savory fruit. It leads us, little by little, toward an evangelized existence through the Word, heard and received.

Reflection Questions

Gazing on the crucifix of St. Damian transforms Clare. In turn, our ears are solicited. What are your obstacles to listening and to a fruitful reception of the Word? Where are your privileged places of meeting with the Word? Try remembering the words received, which are a good fruit or a rose and which surprise you and help you to live.

11
Become Love

Focus Point

///////////////

It is in daily and fraternal life that the Word, heard and prayed, will find the good earth to bring forth fruit. Though not chosen, the sister and the other one are a gift of God to welcome and to love like the Word. To nourish and cherish cultivates the relational life and expresses the unique value of each person. The task is delicate, is threatened by selfishness and the will for power. But forgiveness, always offered, resurrects the wounded life. Love, then, becomes the light burden, the yoke that Jesus gives to us in order to convert us together in the inexpressible charity of God.

///////////////

And loving one another with the love of Christ,
may you demonstrate without in your deeds
the love you have within so that, compelled by

such an example, the sisters may always grow in the love of God and in mutual charity.

I also beg that (sister) who will be in an office of the sisters to strive to exceed the others more by her virtues and holy life than by her office, so that, stimulated by her example, they obey her not so much because of her office as because of love. Let her also be farsighted and discerning toward her sisters, as a good mother is toward her daughters, and let her especially take care to provide for them according to the needs of each one out of the alms that the Lord shall give. Let her also be so kind and affable that they may securely reveal their needs and confidently have recourse to her at any hour, as they see fit both for themselves as well as for their sisters. Let the sisters who are subject, however, keep in mind that, for the sake of God, they have given up their own wills. Therefore I want them to obey their mother of their own free will as they have promised the Lord, so that, seeing their charity, humility, and unity they have toward one another, she might bear all the burdens of her office more lightly, and what is painful and bitter might be changed into sweetness through their way of life.

(TestCl 59–70)

*T*he mystery of God, contemplated on the face of the Crucified and his provoking Word welcomed with passion, led Clare to a very concrete action. In conforming her whole being to Jesus and in allowing her *inexpressible love* to irrigate it, she herself becomes a "mirror" of Love. The gaze of Jesus which has absorbed her own and the words of the Living One which have captivated her ears, now inscribe in her heart the traces of the divine tenderness and mercy.

A Present from God

You, mutually cherishing the same love of Christ.... The relational life is the privileged compost where God-Love is able to be experienced and touched. It is there that we discover his compassion for each of his creatures, and there that we learn how we can, in our turn, love him.

The other is a gift offered to our liberty to love. Clare has a very vivid understanding of it. She will evoke in her *Testament*: the *sisters that the Lord had given me shortly after my own conversion* (*TestCl* 25). She has received them from the prodigality of the *Father of Mercies* in order to create with them a living together in simplicity and poverty, nourished from the love and the mercy with which they love Jesus. The love is expressed in the authenticity of the daily gestures and a tender affection. The respect and the wonder before the other, characterizes Clare's evangelical gaze. They allow us to escape the indifference born of habit and the wear and tear of time which will risk "treating as a mere object" those whom life gives us as companions on the road.

To Nourish and Cherish

Clare remains concerned to express exteriorly the sentiments of her heart accorded to each sister belonging to God: *For if a mother loves and cares for her child according to the flesh, how much more attentively should a sister love and care for her sister according to the Spirit? (RegCl* 8:16).

The love of Christ, ineffable and superabundant, is poured out through the clay vases of our lives. Goodness, discretion and foresight are translated in the course of the hours, day and night, by the solicitude of Clare for each of her sisters. Every fraternal gesture, even the most elementary, most humble and most simple can become "full" with maternal attention and with diligent care dwelling in the heart.

How do we live differently *the unity of hearts in mutual love (RegCl* 10:7) and allow the *Father of Mercies* to take maternal care of us? Clare knows it: it is not enough to break bread to share it, to draw water to quench the thirst, to relieve the suffering or to wash the feet. It is also necessary to provide an indispensable and precious nourishment to nourish the heart which expresses the unique value of each person. In her solicitude, full of delicateness, she asks those who will succeed her *to console the afflicted sisters* and to be *the last refuge of those who are troubled* (*RegCl* 4:11–12). Through her, the compassion of the Father raises up the wounded life which is dying from the struggle.

To Pardon

This love, key of the arch of every relational life and stronger than our fascination or our natural repulsions, is not lived in an idyllic manner. If Clare proposes a form of life where neither the precedence nor the forceful relations exists, the daily life very rapidly reveals the human weakness and the sin which still hampers the progress *on the path of prudent happiness* (*2LAg* 13). A realist, she denounces the desire of domination and the possessor instinct which wounds love: *I admonish and exhort in the Lord Jesus Christ to beware of all pride, vainglory, envy, avarice, care and anxiety about this world, detraction and murmuring, dissension and division* (*RegCl* 10:6).

Only forgiveness allows us to begin again. The mutual love which is strengthened in forgiveness and the non-judgment is so precious that *the abbess and her sisters, however, must beware not to become angry or disturbed on account of another's sin, for anger and disturbance prevent charity in oneself and in others* (*RegCl* 9:5).

The Light Burden of Love

Clare and her sisters, together, feel responsible for their search of the Lord and of the rootedness of this desire in the darkness of daily life. Nothing is imposed which is not in the service of life and of joy. *In the service of the sisters*, Clare applies herself to foresee the needs of each one. Far from submitting servility, the sisters, *through the love, the humility and the unity that they have among them*, lighten the burden of the abbess, changing *into sweetness that which is wounding and harsh.*

Clare writes: *By carrying each other's burden of charity in this way we will easily fulfill the law of Christ* (*LEr* 17). Is it a clearer echo of the invitation of Jesus: *Shoulder my yoke and learn from me, for I am gentle and humble in heart.... Yes, my yoke is easy and my burden light* (*Mt* 11:29–30). Clare not only asks Ermentrude to carry or support with patience and benevolence the burden of fragility and even the sin of her sisters. She invites her to place herself with her sister, under the yoke of love in order to advance with her on the route of conversion to the charity of God.

The place where the life of communion of the sisters of Saint Damian takes root resembles any situation where we learn to love the other for herself. There exists a thousand and one occasions to create some gestures and words to incarnate the love which nourishes us. As they, we are promised to simple and ordinary tasks which comfort, console, heal, serve and beautify existence. We can open a breach for hope in the disabled hearts and bodies. Thus, the love will always be recognized and loved. It will always trace out a path from person to person.

Reflection Questions

The God-love essentially gives Himself to encounter you in a relationship. Make a strong act of faith when in difficult moments. What is it that enables you to pose loving acts when nothing, humanly speaking, pushes you to do so? What most forcefully stops this movement of love in you? What is your experience of forgiveness?

12
Become Prayer

Focus Point

////////////

The account of the Saracens translates Clare's audacious faith and the strength of her cry to God in distress. This one cannot destroy her because she knows that Jesus is with her in the midst of the storm. She makes God's compassion her own for a wounded humanity. God's burden is hers. In the strength of love, she welcomes the mission to help God and to carry a share of the burden which torments His heart. With Him, she chooses to intercede, to cry and to hope, comforting God and each one of his children in the same movement.

////////////

[The war opposes the troops of the Emperor to those of the Pope. Some soldiers already climbed the wall of the enclosure of the monastery when

Clare comes forward, ill and without any other protection than the ivory pyx containing the Eucharist].

////////////

Clare's biographer recounts: *With tears [in her eyes], she said to Christ: Look, my Lord, do you wish to deliver into the hands of pagans your defenseless servants whom You have nourished with Your own love? Lord, I beg You, defend Your servants whom I am not able to defend at this time. My Lord, she said, please protect this city which for Your love sustains us And the Lord said to her: It will suffer afflictions, but will be defended by my protection.*

Then the virgin, raising her tear-filled face, comforted the weeping [sisters] saying: My dear children, I guarantee, you will not suffer any harm. Just have confidence in Christ. Without delay, the subdued boldness of those dogs began immediately to be alarmed. They were driven away by the power of the one who was praying, departing in haste over those walls which they had scaled (Cel 22).

*W*e have already perceived that the world is not strange to the embrace of Christ and of the Beloved. Much to the contrary, if the poor Crucified carries his gaze on one of us with a look of loving kindness, it is to unveil the profound depths of his compassion toward broken humanity. Clare cannot close herself to that which wounds the Son of man, touched in the depths of her being (*Lk* 10:33) for the misery of her brothers and sisters.

With Jesus, the praying person welcomes all distress which mars the beauty of the world. There in the emptiness, one learns to perceive the scoffed at presence of the *King of Glory,* and there to hear the cry of God deeply moved by human suffering. The passion of the Father and that of humanity is revealed as one and the same mystery of poverty. To contemplate one, is to hear the other knocking at our door. From that time on, it becomes impossible not to enter with Jesus and Clare in a prayer of supplication and a cry of hope toward Easter morning.

The events of Clare's life, narrated above, illustrate this supplication molded in faith and hope.

Cry toward God

All life carries a struggle within it: Struggles with oneself, with others and with God.

The enemies of Assisi are within the walls of Saint Damian.... Today, the *enemy* comes to us under other forms which we must drive out. He wants to block our growth in liberty and love. Sometimes our confidence in a person as well as in life, finds itself altered.

In the heart of violence, a call remains possible. As the disciples in the heart of the storm

(*Mk* 4:35–41), Clare awakens Jesus. She cannot silence the ardor of charity which burns in her maternal heart (cf. *4LAg* 5). A cry in the name of humanity threatened by suffering and death, constrained by force in their fundamental rights, her prayer rejoins the compassion of God. But it is the night. Often the only response is the bottomless silence of an absence which torments the heart and the spirit. Therefore, faith, hope and love remain.

Far from being disheartened by the promised struggle, Clare carries Christ into the center of the event. For her, the mystery of the Incarnation is not a theory, but the truest reality in the middle of our distressed moments. The place of the Lord Jesus, under the humble appearance of bread, is truly there in our midst. The humility of the real presence in the Eucharist is not perplexing to Clare.

To Help God

By contemplating the poor Christ and strong in her unique confidence in the Father, Clare makes his compassion and his cry of intercession her own. In her fragility, she is assured of being strong from the victorious might of his Passover. Thus, powerless and weakened by illness, she has no fear to be placed between the enemy and her sisters. Not alone, because Christ is with her. Him in her, she becomes a

wall and protection for the sheep that were con-
fided to her: *My sisters and my daughters, do not
fear because the Lord will defend you. I wish to be
your ransom; if it should happen that the enemies
come down to the monastery, place me before them*
(*PC* IV:14).

To cry to the Lord is to be in solidarity; it
is, in our turn, to enter into the mystery of the
Incarnation of the Son who did not spare his
pain in order to be with those who suffer and
die. Likewise, our weakness can be placed at
their service. The prayer of intercession places
us, like watchers in the breach and on the bor-
ders, there where life and death meet face to
face. *They will never fall silent, day or night. No
peace for you, as you keep Yahweh's attention!* says
the Prophet (*Is* 62:6).

Clare asks to be placed in front of the enemy
with the humble sign of Bread, the Body of the
Lord Jesus, as her only refuge. *By the virtue of
faith, she has taken hold of* (*3LAg* 7) this presence
which paradoxically saves us, in accepting a
powerlessness similar to our own, before the
mortal chasms which lie in wait for us. Clare
understands that to become a *helper* of God and
allow his infinite compassion for everyone to
vibrate in her, there is no other route than to
enter with him in the humility of love which
disarms every form of power and violence: *You
are a co-worker of God Himself and a support for the*

weak members of His ineffable Body (*3LAg* 8). Only the praying person with a poor heart can allow herself to be clothed with the grace of compassion and of intercession. She sees herself entrusted with the mission to help God by receiving the part which comes back to her of the burden of his mercy. She can turn her supplication toward him with confidence and love, espouse his blazing tenderness, both maternal and paternal toward a world which gives birth in suffering. To intercede is a battle. The humble person dares to undertake it because of a certitude in God and relies on his promise. In a confidence and an abandon without limits, Clare does not hesitate to recall to the Lord her love. *He calls me and I answer him: In distress I am at his side.* Who pronounces this verse of Psalm 90? The praying person? God? Both, without doubt, because they have need of each other in order to awaken hope in the human heart.

Our supplication draws its audacity in the identical words of Jesus: *Be courageous: I have conquered the world* (*Jn* 16:33). *No one can steal anything from the Father's hand* (*Jn* 10:29).

I will always protect you ... In the besieged cloister of Saint Damian, as on our routes of Emmaus, He walks with us, Him, *your helper and the best consoler* (*LEr* 16). With Him, it is ours to bring about the fulfillment of every intercession by opening *a gateway of hope* (*Ho* 2:17) in place of dead ends.

Reflection Questions

Have you already lived this cry toward God when there was darkness in your life? for yourself? for humanity? What enables you to persevere in prayer? To strengthen your faith? "To help God." What a paradox! Are you in agreement with this approach of a poor and fragile God? If it is necessary "to help him," what becomes of his infinite power? Does the promise of Jesus, to always watch over you, have an influence on you?

13
Become Free

Focus Point

///////////////

Clare cannot tolerate any obstacle in her journey.
Freely, she moves forward toward her goal. Sharing
in the life of the poor Crucified is her daily life and
her horizon. Neither anything nor any person can
divert her from this proposal. She moves liberated
from all interior and exterior riches. Far from being
self-satisfied and arrogant, this liberty leads her to
overcome the temptation of the rupture. She lives
in the Church, humble and respectful, attached to
the poor Christ. This liberty allows her to take risks
because she knows that she is bonded forever to the
One who freed her.

///////////////

In all of this, follow the counsel of our vener-
able father, our Brother Elias, the Minister
General, that you may walk more securely in

*the way of the commands of the Lord. Prize
it beyond the advice of the others and cherish
it as dearer to you than any gift. If anyone
has said anything else to you or suggested any
other thing to you that might hinder your perfection or that would seem contrary to your
divine vocation even though you must respect
him, do not follow his counsel. As a poor virgin embrace the poor Christ.*

*Look upon Him who became contempt-
ible in this world for you, and follow Him,
making yourself contemptible in this world
for Him. Most noble Queen, gaze, consider,
contemplate, desiring to imitate Your Spouse.*

*[Who] though more beautiful than the
children of men became, for your salvation,
the lowest of men, was despised, struck,
scourged untold times throughout His entire
body, and then died amid the suffering of
the cross.*

(2LAg 15–20)

////////////

L ove for the poor Christ places Clare standing with the full stature of a free woman,
who hears in the depths of her being a call to
live the most radical poverty according to the
Gospel. If she holds her life in her hands, it is to
be able to give herself totally to the *most beautiful of the children of men.*

Live Freely

Since the day when she recognized poverty as the terrain chosen by God to share our history, Clare no longer wants to desert it. Since the beginning of her vocation, she made proof of an unwavering determination. To affront the social conventions in order to adopt an unknown form of religious life does not happen of itself. She follows her own route, docile to the voice of the Spirit who breathes in her, *this call of God to be perfect.*

Liberty is an unknown word in her vocabulary. But the manner in which she makes her choices, witnesses to the gift that God gives her. In our era, marked by the concern of personal flowering, Clare teaches us how to assume our "yes" and our "no" in order to reach the full stature of Christ. Her love toward God unfolds all her potentiality, adjusts it to the desire of her Lord, in order for a response to spring forth without ambiguity and to break new ground in the liberty of the Spirit. Neither contesting society nor rebellious, she simply selects what the Wisdom of God gives her to perceive as the just, the true and the good. Without hesitation, she engages herself in truth, without looking back and risking the indispensable options.

Not having goods to defend, Clare advances, free from the legitimate fears which assail the proprietor's instinct. Liberty frees from a rigid and strained asceticism, which counts "to merit" her

happiness. She removes the anguish of wanting
to succeed in her life as well as the ceaseless recur-
ring anxiety before the burden of the future. She
is free from the worry of accumulating securities
and goods in order to protect herself from their
lack and from suffering. In the rhythm of our consent, liberty fashions the poor heart in stripping
it of interior and exterior riches which encumber
it. In return, the poor Gospel person no longer
knows the fear of losing it. Her true treasure is
set in the heavens, there where the worms can not
destroy, where the robbers neither break through
nor steal it (*Mt* 6:19–21).

In Communion

In a Church, paralyzed by power and riches,
Clare places her security in the Father, who takes
care of the birds of the heaven and the lilies of
the fields. Pure folly, the Popes and Bishops
will judge with an unsettled prudence! In their
affection for Clare, they experience much pity
more than once before the precariousness of
the material existence of the sisters. The Pope
wanted to persuade her to accept some posses-
sions: *"If you fear for your vow, we will absolve you
from it."* To which she retorted: *"Holy Father, I
will never in any way wish to be absolved from the
following of Christ"* (*Cel* 14).

Clare does not hesitate to lead Agnes of
Prague in the audacious Gospel liberty: *If anyone
has said anything else to you or suggested any other*

thing to you that might hinder your perfection or that would seem contrary to your divine vocation, even though you must respect him, do not follow his counsel (2LAg 17). However, she never yields to the temptation of a rupture. The Church remains the community where she lives her faith and in which she receives the Word and Bread for the road. She wants to be faithful to Jesus in a communion of responsible obedience. The folly of poverty comes into collision with a very comprehensible wisdom which would turn back from this call. But Clare draws, within the good fortune to follow Christ, the tranquil strength to resist — even to oppose — in order to persevere in her desire. With respect and patience, she lives in the Church, open to the solicitude of her Shepherds in this regard, but attentive so that the inspiration of the Spirit is never stifled.

For an Indefectible Attachment

With strength, Clare insists with Agnes: *As a poor virgin, embrace the poor Christ!* The ultimate aim, expressed in a concise and exceptional manner, is that all the audacity of faith and of love of the Poor Sister of Assisi is transmitted!

It is urgent to remove the obstacles and to keep the momentum in the race undertaken, that nothing any longer separates the poor heart from the *poor Crucified....* Their embrace becomes their most precious good; the attachment which binds them to each other and the expression of their most high liberty. For to what good, the liberty, if it is not to give itself in love? She takes the audacity to allow herself to be led by an Other (*Jn* 21:18), to enter in her project and to do everything possible in order to accomplish it.

Love unveils our true personality. It accomplishes this through the liberty of the gift, which alone can respond to the attractiveness of the poor and humble countenance of God, brought about in us. This is the paradox which Clare discovers and lives: only the *Most High Son of God*, washing the feet of the disciples (*Jn* 13), breaks away from all slavery and all fear. The image of the dying Christ in destitution, humiliation and contempt, leaves a footprint of fire in her. All her simple and unadorned existence carries the imprint. In the roughness or the sweetness of fraternal relationships, throughout the years of illness and in the long drawn out struggle to save the *Privilege of Poverty*, Clare discovers a unique treasure: Jesus Christ came to enrich us through his poverty.

Our search, often tactless, for flowering and happiness sometimes errs by taking the wrong paths through the fields. Our attachment to Jesus can be born from the sovereign liberty of the Gospel, even when our sensibility rebels at the prospect of uniting ourselves to the *poor Crucified*.

The Good News contests a liberty which would only be a disguised slavery. The call of the Poor One of Nazareth orients the better of our fundamental energies (possession, power and pleasure) within a covenant which binds us to him: *You need to do one thing more. Go ... sell ... come, follow me* (*Mk* 10:21). This liberty is received, then, as the fruit ripened for a long time in the sun of our attachment to Jesus Christ.

Reflection Questions

Are you acquainted with some attitudes of resistance to authority in the Church? What is your relation to the Church as an institution? In the event of conflicts, what is the price to pay to remain in communion? Liberty is a path, but to what? What supports it? What shackles it? Have you experienced attachments which free you?

14
Become Life

Focus Point

////////////

Clare celebrates life, life received, of which she knows the source. This life is her most invaluable good, to keep, to return in a song of praise and in offering to the Source of all good. The usual ascetic regulations are there only to deploy all the capacities to love with common sense and wisdom. The desire for life requires us "to live well" and this wish, full of a solid pragmatism for her friend, Agnes, resounds as an invitation to create all of her being as a living praise to God.

////////////

But our flesh is not bronze, nor is our strength that of stone, rather we are frail and inclined to every bodily weakness. I beg you, therefore, dearly beloved, to refrain wisely and prudently from an indiscreet austerity in the

*fasting that you have undertaken. And I beg
you in the Lord to praise the Lord by your
very life, to offer the Lord your reasonable
service and your sacrifice always seasoned
with salt. May you do well in the Lord,
as I hope I do myself, and, in your holy
prayers, remember me along with my sisters.*

(*3LAg* 38–42)

////////////

*T*his is an astonishing counsel to a friend
who wishes to be converted. At once,
it witnesses to the well-balanced solicitude of
Clare for Agnes, of her profound wisdom and
of her common sense.

Celebrate the Source

The essential proposition of Clare is to
acknowledge the Lord, to recognize and admire
him in his truth and to celebrate the beauty of
his love in words and actions. From him whom
she has experienced gentleness, she proclaims
his goodness and wisdom with her whole being.
Centered on the voluntary deprivation to which
he has consented in order to rejoin in the roots of
its being, she has only words of gratitude for him.
All that he has said, made and suffered for her
and for the world is included in her thanksgiving.
In a cry of amazement, bursts forth her visceral
need to bless, to praise and to be grateful to the

one who comes to her under humble appearances and in the fullness of *his inexpressible love.*

In beginning, we already evoked this moment where, during the vigil of the death of Clare, the delightful exclamation bursts forth from her heart; where her confession of the Lord, unfolding throughout her life, is accomplished in its plenitude: *Blessed are you O Lord, You who have created me.*

Praise and blessing overflow, respiration of her soul and breath which enlarges it. *Since the Lord has called us to such great things that those who are a mirror and example to others may be reflected in us, we are greatly bound to bless and praise God and to be strengthened more and more to do good in the Lord* (*TestCl* 21–22).

This is her unique task: to become praise, a free woman who receives all from the Lord and returns every good toward its Source. But how is it possible to bind together the happiness of living and sacrifice?

Alive, Confess the Lord

Clare seems to take some distance in comparison with the habitual ascetic prescriptions for the religious life of her time. In her own life of penance, nevertheless, it happened that her common sense and her realism failed. Her personal excess led her to imprudence. But the very alive consciousness of her first call to praise God helps her to put in perspective the means to use to keep love awakened. She chose for her sisters, discernment and wisdom, bringing a very maternal attention to their health. God is the God of the living. He desires us to be partners of a covenant where, risen in received and shared love, we become capable of ordering the values which make us live and grow in the recognition of the Source who gives us existence.

To live to praise our Creator opens the true liberty in which we become truly living in his image and resemblance. To persevere on the path, to always enter with more good fortune in the original chant of admiration and of thanks of the living to the Living, it is not necessary to force the body — nor the soul — to the "deadly" renouncements! *But our flesh is not bronze, nor is our strength that of stone, rather, we are frail and inclined to every bodily weakness!* The Lord awaits neither our sacrifices nor holocausts (*Os* 6:6); He prefers mercy and justice from a heart which gives with joy. Very often we aspire to offer him the offering of our choice. We do not lack imagination when we want to purify our desire and mark the opening of our being to God who alone is good. The happy discovery of our generosity can abound, but our manner of acting, does it not often appear *without either moderation or realism*? The Lord is happy to repeat to us: *Look, today I am offering you life and prosperity, death and disaster.... Choose life, then* (*Dt* 30:15–20).

With an infinite respect in regard to his creature, he humanizes us, teaching us to love our
body within which we breathe his living breath.
It is a question of living to love, to praise in a
reasonable service, and that in the interior of our
weaknesses itself.

An excessive preoccupation regarding the
offering that we can make to please the Lord
pollutes the simplicity of our heart by centering
us on ourselves and on our gifts with the risk
of forgetting to whom we offer them. Perhaps
asceticism essentially consists in having a bal-
anced vigilance and common sense toward the
precious gift of health which allows praise to
flash across the weighty earth of our humanity.

Be Well

In recalling to us the ultimate aim of our life
which is to sing of God, Clare sends us back to
the body, a humble instrument placed at our disposition and upon which we play beautiful music.

Austerity is not necessarily the sign of an
authentic spiritual life. The gifts of God are
not measured by our own momentum, even
the most generous. They are purely gratuitous
from his part. True and poor before Him, we
enter in a movement of love where respect
and tenderness, gratuitousness and gratitude
intermingle, where the daily life offers itself
as the privileged place of contemplation and
of asceticism, where *holy pure Simplicity has for*

companion Queen Wisdom (SalV 1). Clare affirms
with sobriety: praise is not found in the heaven
of her flight in fasting and penances, it bursts
forth in the heart with a full consent of respect
for brother body, in the humor which submits
itself to the reality with wisdom. What does
fasting matter, if it is not rooted in thanksgiving where the heart breathes the loving liberty
of God. The desire to live for God imposes
the choice to live *well,* to dwell among those
capable of receiving from an Other and to give
oneself in return. Praise is the righteousness of
the poor heart, freed from all ascetic preoccupation. Praise helps us to discover things and
to visit all beings with a expanded heart of
unbounded gratitude. *When Clare used to send the
serving sisters outside the monastery, she reminded
them to praise God when they saw beautiful trees,
flowers, and bushes; and, likewise, always to praise
Him for and in all things when they saw people and
creatures (Pr XIV: 9).*

Be well, confess the goodness of the Lord by
seasoning your asceticism and your renouncements with a grain of wisdom. Dispossession
of self in thanksgiving is a sign of spiritual
health. Adjust your fasting and privations
according to your fragility and your corporal
weaknesses. Because the living, the living,
alone praise the Lord of life today (*Is* 38:19).

Reflection Questions

How can asceticism be in the service of
Life? When is it trapped? What connection do
you find between spiritual health and physi-
cal health? "A happy sobriety": what does this
expression evoke for you? What makes you a
truly living human being, standing happy and
free? If God awaits a life of praise from you, in
what must you be vigilant?

15
Become Blessing

Focus Point

////////////

In the Book of Genesis, God blesses us first; he wants the good for each one of his creatures. We can live surrounded by benevolent forces, wrapped in his benevolent will.

Clare is held in the current of this goodness without limits and this original blessing comes through to spread it around her.

Thus, the air of the Kingdom is given us to breathe in a new communion with God, others and oneself. This harmony offered to us is the treasure of a free and poor heart which never ceases to walk humbly with God, who is always very near.

////////////

To you, my sisters and my daughters,
And to all the others who come and remain
in your company

both now and in the future,
who have persevered until the end in every
other monastery of the Poor Ladies.

I, Clare, a handmaid of Christ, a little plant
of our most holy father Francis, a sister and
mother of you and the other poor sisters,
although unworthy, bless you during my
life and after my death, as I am able, out of
all the blessings, with which the Father of
mercies has blessed and will bless His sons
and daughters in heaven and on earth and a
spiritual father and mother have blessed and
will bless their spiritual sons and daughters.

Always be lovers of your souls and those of
    all your sisters.
And may you always be eager to observe
    what you promised the Lord.
May the Lord always be with you and may
    you always be with Him. Amen.

(BCl 4–6;11–16)

In the Springing Forth of Goodness

*I*n the introduction to our journey of prayer, we presented it as a stroll in the interior landscape of Clare. At the end of our journey of prayer, she awaits us with many blessings on her lips and in her heart....

How could it be otherwise? The *Father of Mercies*, to whom she prays and who becomes visible in the thousand gestures of daily life, is the inexhaustible Source of all good. From her goodwill for each of her children, Clare becomes the witness. This which she has experienced of the *All Good*, who is her Lord and Creator, becomes the treasure of all. As she, each being and the whole universe are the object of the blessing of the Father.

Because, long before we bless Him, God, blesses us first. Often the bitter realities of our lives render us deaf to His cry of wonder on the first morning of the world: *God saw all that he had made and indeed it was very good* (*Gn* 1:31). God the Living, who gives himself, blesses us at each new dawn. He says it; He wants only the good with respect to everyone. His blessing is our salvation, because in it we receive joy each morning and the strength for the road in the certitude of his fidelity.

Transformed in the image of the One that we love and contemplate, we become witnesses to the whole of divine generosity. And not only exterior witnesses of His blessing, but in our turn, we become sources, *spiritual fathers and mothers,* for those who have been given to us to love. The fecundity of the *Father of Mercies* does not stop at our own heart; it is extended to a multitude through us.

According to Clare, it is our task and our unique preoccupation to which all other activities must be subordinate: *The sisters should desire above all else: to have the Spirit of the Lord and Its holy activity* (*RegCl* 10:9). The vivifying Spirit wants to feel free in our dwelling, awaken us to the true life and through us, to engender other living beings who know the value that they have in the Father's eyes. Some men and women perceive in his gaze the beauty of their existence, even though they have passed through sufferings and nights.

In Search of Harmony

Always be lovers of your souls and those of all your sisters (*and of God*, adds one manuscript). The all gratuitous goodness of the Father, who blesses us and turns His face toward us, leads us toward a profound reconciliation with ourselves and with others. It is not a question of denying the shadows of our lives, these places in our personal history that we would prefer to see rejoin the forgotten spaces in our unconscious, but of which we secretly keep the traces in our everyday behavior. When the gaze of Love is focused on our existence to say that: "It is good; it is very good," we feel welcomed and respected in our whole human adventure marked by the pock-marks of trials. This gaze which blesses us brings us to the simple welcome of who we are. We begin to consent to our true image without mask or a shell. Thus, to be able to connect the joy of thanks with our reconciled being: *O Lord, may You be blessed, Who have created me*. This first fundamental blessing, addressed to the Father,

changes our own gaze. We discover the harmony of everything and of every being in the
"yes" placed upon them by the Creator's original goodness.

In our turn, we enter in the blessing's benevolent current. In the course of time, it becomes
a presence of friendship in humanity close to us
and to our human brothers and sisters. Clare's
heritage to us is her gaze which rejoices in the
existence of the other without reducing it to
that which she already knows. Each morning,
her heart marvels anew at the traces of a loving
image which sketches the icon of her Beloved.

Prayer rooted in the goodness of God takes
hold of the persons and the things bathed in
the ever gratuitous love of the *Father of Mercies*.
It responds in echo to his blessing, making rise
toward him *every blessing*, the song of the poor
fulfilled by divine friendship. The chant which
rejoins the jubilation of Jesus in the hour where
he sees the name of his friends inscribed in the
heavens: *I bless you, Father* (*Mt* 11:25).

Where is Your God

*May the Lord always be with you and may
you always be with Him.*

Let us recollect the final wishes of Clare to
her sisters and to each of us in relation to our
journey of prayer. In our resting places close to
the Lord, Clare believes the only goal is to hollow

out in us a desire for communion with the *Father of Mercies, the poor Christ and the Spirit of the Lord.* In the rhythmic seasons of our spiritual life and in the humility of our very ordinary tasks, we discover a proximity to God who becomes a beggar for our love. He does not establish his dwelling in the vague and fragile horizon of our dreams, but in the rocky and fertile earth of our personal and collective history.

As Clare, we can know the sweet, patient and peaceful joy of a daily companionship with God. Because in the density of ordinary time, under the rainbow of events, the elevation of the music of the Spirit leads us to contemplate the God of promises of whom the creating Word upholds our existence.

To be always with him, as he dwells without end with us.... In this reciprocal blessing bursting forth in the heart of a mutual amazement, we already breathe the air of the Kingdom in us according to the benevolent will of the Lord who wants us to be in a communion of love with Him in every place and in all times. Because there is neither any place nor any time, that is too restricted to live in search of his face.

The voluntary deprivation and the simplicity of daily life with its joys and its pains, such is our "Saint Damian" where in the following of Clare and of her sisters we allow ourselves to be encountered by the *poor Crucified.* There where he invites us to meet him, which is to say in every dwelling of human poverty where a brother or sister celebrates life, loves, suffers and dies.

Keep back nothing of yourself, say "yes" to the God Source, who says "yes" to us, agree to each encountered being as he is, there is our treasure. The riches of the walker, who in the course of the hike being stripped of baggage, has the heart enriched through encounters. The joy of the traveler, surprised to be awaited in the Inn by the stranger who accompanies him on the road.

Reflection Questions

If God blesses me first, how can this Blessing transfigure my life? How do we articulate the love of enemies and prayer? In the face of horror and distress, how can we allow wonderment to become alive? How can we preserve this prayer of wonderment from habit and unsightliness? If God is our day by day companion on the road, what does that really change in our life?

Envoy

Become what you contemplate,
Become the One whom you contemplate.
With the Father and the Holy Spirit,
He blesses you and keeps you.
Go confident, swiftly and joyfully,
You have a good guide for the road,
The poverty of the heart and the fidelity
   of God assure your steps.

Sources to Know Clare of Assisi

Sources

Clare of Assisi. *Early Documents. The Lady*. Revised edition and translation by Regis J. Armstrong, O.F.M. Cap. New York: New City Press, 2006.

Recent Publications

Alberzoni, Maria Pia. *Clare of Assisi and the Poor Sisters in the Thirteenth Century*. Saint Bonaventure, NY: Franciscan Institute Publications, 2004.

Bartoli, Marco. *Clare of Assisi*. Quincy: Franciscan Press, 1993.

_____.*Saint Clare: Beyond the Legend*. Cincinnati: Saint Anthony's Messenger Press, 2010.

Carney, Margaret, O.S.F. *The First Franciscan Woman, Clare of Assisi and Her Form of Life*. Quincy: Franciscan Press, 1993.

Frances Teresa, O.S.C. *Living the Incarnation: Praying with Francis and Clare of Assisi*. London : Darton, Longman and Todd, 1993.

_____.*This Living Mirror: Reflections on Clare of Assisi*. Maryknoll: Orbis Books, 1995.

Godet-Calogeras, Jean-François, editor. *An Unencumbered Heart. A Tribute to Clare of Assisi: 1253–2003.* St. Bonaventure, NY: Franciscan Institute Publications, 2004.

Goorbergh, Edith A. van den, O.S.C. and Theodore H. Zweerman, O.F.M. *Light Shining through a Veil: On Saint Clare's Letters to Saint Agnes of Prague.* Translated by Aline Looman-Graaskamp et Frances Teresa, O.S.C. Leuven: Peeters, 2000.

Ledoux, *Claire Marie. Clare of Assisi: her Spirituality Revealed in her Letters.* St. Anthony Messenger Press: ©2003.

Miller, Ramona, O.S.F. *In the Footsteps of Saint Clare: A Pilgrim's Guide Book.* St. Bonaventure: The Franciscan Institute, 1993.

Miller, Ramona, O.S.F. and Ingrid Peterson, O.S.F. *Praying with Clare of Assisi.* Winona, MN: Saint Mary's Press, Christian Brothers Publications, 2002.

Peterson, Ingrid J., O.S.F. *Clare of Assisi: A Biographical study.* Quincy: Franciscan Press, 1993.

Schneider, Herbert, O.F.M., *Contemplation in the Spirit of Clare of Assisi.* Rome: Curia Generale dei Frati Minori, [1994].

St. Paul, Mary, P.C.C., *Clothed with Gladness: The Story of St. Clare.* Huntington, IN: Our Sunday Visitor Publishing Division, 2000.

Also available in the
"15 Days of Prayer" series:

Saint Benedict *(André Gozier)*
978-1-56548-304-0, paper

Saint Bernadette of Lourdes *(François Vayne)*
978-1-56548-314-9, paper

Dietrich Bonhoeffer *(Matthieu Arnold)*
978-1-56548-311-8, paper

Saint Catherine of Siena *(Chantal van der
    Plancke and Andrè Knockaert)*
978-156548-310-1, paper

Saint Clare of Assisi *(Marie-France Becker)*
978-1-56548-371-2

The Curé of Ars *(Pierre Blanc)*
978-0764-807138, paper

Saint Dominic *(Alain Quilici)*
978-0764-807169, paper

Saint Katharine Drexel *(Leo Luke Marcello)*
978-0764-809231, paper

Saint Faustina Kowalska *(John J. Cleary)*
978-1-56548-350-7, paper

Charles de Foucauld *(Michael Lafon)*
978-0764-804892, paper

Saint Francis de Sales *(Claude Morel)*
978-0764-805752, paper

Saint Francis of Assisi *(Thaddée Matura)*
978-1-56548-315-6, paper

Saint Jeanne Jugan *(Michel Lafon)*
978-1-56548-329-3, paper

Saint John of the Cross *(Constant Tonnelier)*
978-0764-806544, paper

Saint Eugene de Mazenod *(Bernard Dullier)*
978-1-56548-320-0, paper

Thomas Merton *(André Gozier)*
978-1-56548-330-9

Henri Nouwen *(Robert Waldron)*
978-1-56548-324-8, paper

**Saint Martín de Porres: A Saint of the
    Americas** *(Brian J. Pierce)*
978-0764-812163, paper

Meister Eckhart *(André Gozier)*
978-0764-806520, paper

Brother Roger of Taizé *(Sabine Laplane)*
978-1-56548-349-1, paper

Saint Elizabeth Ann Seton *(Betty Ann McNeil)*
978-0764-808418, paper

Pierre Teilhard de Chardin *(André Dupleix)*
978-0764-804908, paper

Saint Teresa of Avila *(Jean Abiven)*
978-1-56548-366-8, paper

Saint Thomas Aquinas *(André Pinet)*
978-0764-806568, paper

Saint Vincent de Paul *(Jean-Pierre Renouard)*
978-1-56548-357-6